ABOVE THE CLOUDS ...

WINNING STRATEGIES

FROM 30,000 FEET

To all the financial professionals who work tirelessly every day to secure our clients' life savings and retirement income: Whether you are in a home office manufacturing products or providing post-sale service, thank you for giving hundreds of thousands of us professionals the tools necessary to make a difference for so many people. To the independent or career agents, and financial advisors who miss dinners with their family so other families can be more secure in their retirement: thank you for your service to our industry and to the billions of Americans you serve.

I want to thank the generous contributions of Norma Endersby and her Creative Services team at Ash Brokerage. They provide the support necessary to carry out these communications with ease. Thanks to Sheryl Brown for pushing me to be a consistent blogger, which is the genesis of this book. Special thanks goes to Tami Brigle for editing all of my writings after business trips. It's unfortunate for her that Fort Wayne, Indiana, has few direct flights, so her work is doubled every business trip with a connecting flight. Also, Megen Gaylord needs special recognition as Annuity Concierge and assistant at Ash Brokerage. She coordinates all my writings through our social media outlets and allows me to concentrate on the topics that remain timely and, hopefully, impactful to our readers and followers.

Finally, travel carries its costs. I want to thank my wife, Alisa, for always supporting me and loving me, even when I am not always present. She has adjusted her life immensely as we combined our lives in the summer of 2015. I am proud of her as she chases her dream that will impact our communities. She will always be my inspiration.

Good Selling,

Mike

Contents

Foreword

By CJ McClanahan - Speaker, Author, Executive Coach

In case you've never been on the receiving end of a meeting with a financial planner, let me tell you how it typically feels from the client's perspective.

You enter a beautiful office and are immediately greeted by a polite receptionist who offers your choice of coffee, water or soda. Moments later, you are led into a luxurious conference room where you meet your finely dressed financial advisor.

He/she then slides you a bound presentation filled with charts/ graphs illustrating your current financial situation and proposed changes for the future. Approximately 17 minutes later, your eyes have glazed over and, if you're like me, you're ready to offer your advisor $500 to cut the meeting short.

No matter how much research an advisor puts into planning for the meeting, all most people hear is "market fluctuation, blah, blah, interest bearing accounts, blah, blah, mitigate risk, blah …" All we want to hear is "You beat the market and have more money than before."

That's it.

In all fairness, financial advisors have the extremely difficult task of digesting tons of complex pieces of information into a simple summary that needs to be absorbed by an emotional client who probably checks their email every 3 minutes.

The simple truth is that there's too much information for any one person to comprehend. The most seasoned financial professional struggles to wrap their arms around all the investment terms and options in the marketplace, much less communicate these concepts to a client.

It's an extremely difficult job.

That's why it's so refreshing to run into someone like Mike McGlothlin.

Mike doesn't give financial advice; he educates with stories. He recognizes that the average person doesn't really care about "fixed annuities" – they want to feel secure that they are making the right decisions.

He takes dry and confusing material and makes it interesting, inspiring his readers to pay attention.

Reading Mike's work will feel like having a conversation with a good friend. He'll you put you at ease by relating a complex concept to something you do every day, and he closes each piece with a quick summary that captures the essence of his message in just a few words.

There's a reason Mike's so good at connecting with the average investor and financial professional – he's obsessed with constant improvement.

I've worked with hundreds of executives in my career and most are committed to growing their top lines, but few want to put in the work required to improve themselves.

Mike is a true outlier.

He's always looking for an edge, whether it's from a book, workshop or podcast. He understands that building a successful business starts with mastering your ability to understand and communicate a value proposition.

And, no matter how good he gets, he never stops focusing on the next skill he needs to develop.

If you're interested in reading a 2,800 word essay written by a Ph.D. whose goal is to impress you with their vocabulary, this book may not be for you.

However, if you're interested in a comfortable journey filled with digestible bits of insights, I encourage you to read on.

Part I

Retirement Income Strategies

Thoughts from Mike

What is the Cost of Income?

August 13, 2015

Have you ever thought about the true cost of income? Too often, we simply take the current payout percentage and divide that into the required annual income to find a solution. But, are we really helping the client understand the cost of generating income? Or, are we even doing the client justice by simplifying the solution with the hottest income rider?

In reality, clients need to consider many factors as they transition from asset accumulation to asset consumption for the rest of their lives. As advisors, we must create a strategy that provides a minimum level of income the client will not outlive. So many of us stop after completing the simple calculation with an income rider. However, there are other considerations.

Planning to minimize the tax impact on income received has a collateral effect on other aspects of the income stream. For example, minimizing taxable income can assist with the taxation of Social Security through the compression of the Modified Adjusted Income calculation. Reducing taxation early in retirement may allow for bracket bumping with Roth conversions for qualified assets.

More importantly, we must deliver income that is adjusted for some level of inflation. Many say inflation is the cruelest tax of all. It is silent; you don't feel it at any particular time of the year, and it is generally in small increments. But, over time, it will reduce the effect on a retiree's buying power. While it is difficult to speculate where inflation will be in 10 or 20 years, there are ways to increase the minimum income level through cost of living increase riders on some products. This should be done in a guaranteed and frequent manner.

Finally, we must consider the impact of fees on the income stream. Too often, we look at a gross number for income. But, as I've said before, it's not what you earn; it's what you keep. A 1 percent fee on a portfolio earning 6 percent reduces the return by 17 percent. As we move to a more transparent environment, discussions with clients will become more important. They're becoming knowledgeable about the impact of fees, so they will look for advisors who will help them keep more of their assets.

Client demand for advice and solutions will remain high, so there has never been a better time to be in the industry. However, we have to think about our efficiency and effectiveness in helping them generate income. Instead of reaching for the easiest solution available in an income rider, I challenge everyone to look at more options.

Winning Strategy: Taxes, inflation and fees can cost your clients a lot of income. Look deeper for solutions to make the client's income more efficient and effective during distribution.

Earning and Keeping Income
February 23, 2015

We work with thousands of advisors across the country, so I see a lot of client statements and financial plans, the overwhelming majority focusing on gross retirement income. However, most Americans don't live on their gross income, they live on what's left over. Or, as I like to remind my clients: It's not what you earn – it's what you keep.

So, when planning for retirement income, we need to look at what the client actually lives on and not what the highest income rider generates. After we determine the actual gap, we can attack it with a solution. Too often, I see the quick fix: "Here's an income rider that meets your guaranteed income need." It's great to meet the client's income need, but did we really look at the best possible solution?

Understanding the tax drag on income payouts allows us to better estimate what the client will actually keep and be able to use for living expenses. If we don't settle for the easy sale, we might look at a combination of tax-advantaged income involving single-premium immediate annuities, deferred income annuities and other lifetime income solutions. Today's products allow you to ladder income with some first-in, first-out taxation and exclusion ratios, while others remain taxed as last-in, first-out.

More importantly, we can stagger income with the least amount of tax impact during life phases with the most income need. As Social Security increases, required minimum distributions and other income sources begin; fee and tax implications can be reduced with proper planning.

When the next income planning case comes across your desk, take a look at the tax impact of the proposed income solution. If the client wants more money for living expenses, think about leveraging annuities for reducing the tax drag on the income portfolio.

Winning Strategy: It's not what you earn or what the income rider generates … It's what the client gets to keep that matters.

Make a Game Plan to Remove Risks
November 26, 2015

As a former student basketball manager at Indiana University, I remember listening to Coach Bob Knight talking to his assistants about strategy. Typically, the game plan revolved around taking away a strength for the opposing team – or taking away a risk to our team. Reducing a significant risk greatly increased our chances of winning.

Why don't we do the same with our clients?

Maybe we don't know the risks for each client. After all, there are so many risks associated with retirement planning. In order to best serve our clients, we look holistically at tax consequences, cash flow, charitable and gifting strategies, survivor's income protection techniques, and maximizing Social Security. Risk mitigation strategies like long-term care and life insurance are usually discussed, but not necessarily as urgently as they should. To a lesser extent, we address inflation, housing and health care concerns for retirees.

All those risk are important; however, there is one risk that multiplies all the above risks: longevity. If your clients run out of money, several things can happen at once:

- Cash flow becomes strained due to a reliance on government provided programs
- Maintaining income to a survivor becomes nearly impossible with few alternatives, as past Social Security decisions can't be changed
- Long-term care (at the level of care the client deserves) becomes burdensome and can create emotional conflict due to the financial stress

One way to alleviate the exponential impact of any of these risks is to address longevity up front. Planning for a guaranteed, inflation-adjusted floor of income should be the cornerstone of any retirement planning strategy. Additionally, the risk of longevity can only be shifted to insurance products that provide income you can't outlive.

Regardless of net worth or total assets, your clients should never self-insure their longevity. Because the risk of longevity isn't a singular impact. It's a risk that impacts their entire net worth.

Winning Strategy: Make a game plan for eliminating your clients' biggest risks by addressing longevity first. Start their retirement income strategy with guaranteed, inflation-adjusted income with a life contingency. By taking longevity off the table, you increase their probability of success in retirement.

The New ROI

September 10, 2015

Business schools still teach ROI, I'm sure. For most Americans, unfortunately, it might be the wrong ROI.

Business schools are probably stuck on the traditional "Return On Investment," and I can argue that many financial planners are still talking to their clients about the same thing. However, I say the new ROI is, "Reliability Of Income." Because for most retirees, the need for a steady, dependable, lifetime income continues to grow in importance.

So many planners and schools focus on the returns of a portfolio. In reality, the changes in return from 5 percent to 6 percent, for example, have a nominal difference on the retiree's income outcome. Now, the sequencing of those returns, especially early in retirement, may have a larger effect on the outcome. But overall averages will not impact the success or failure of a retirement plan. Instead, the larger impact comes from life expectancy, which is a variable we cannot predict.

Therefore, clients need to have a guaranteed, inflation-adjusted floor of dependable income in their portfolio. Without it, the success of their retirement portfolio can't be projected accurately. Too many variables – like return on investments, life expectancy, sequencing of returns, health care costs and emergencies – could impact the probability of success.

By focusing on the reliability of their income, clients can reduce the risks in their retirement portfolio. Inflation can be mitigated with cost-of-living increases. Longevity can be eliminated with lifetime income options – both single and joint. Fee and tax drag can be greatly reduced, if not eliminated, by proper choice of product.

Winning Strategy: Put first things first when designing a portfolio – reliability of income should be the new ROI.

What's Your Distribution Rate When It Really Matters?
December 3, 2015

Let's face it. Many of us have short attention spans. Whether it's looking at our phones or tablets, quickly changing conversations with multiple people, or simply not being able to focus on a task, technology and social pressures have changed the way we interact with people and weakened our ability to pay attention for long periods of time.

I feel we tend to keep a shorter vision on retirement planning as well. And, this could be dangerous for our clients.

We talk a lot about life expectancies increasing, and determining the proper payout for a client's assets. Unfortunately, I see many people making plans based upon life expectancies of newborns. We need to concentrate and look at the expanding life expectancies of 65-year-olds and the complications that those extra years bring.

Rising income needs due to inflationary pressures are greatest in retirement because of health care and housing issues. Longer retirements cannot withstand level income for long periods of time, especially with a volatile base of assets. As planners, we need to consider the impacts of our clients' income sources in 20 years, not just in that initial five- to 10-year period.

Over the years, the 4 percent distribution rule has been kicked around by many industry professionals and academics. Again, I don't think the distribution percentage at age 65 is as important as what the percentage will be in 15 years. Too often, we set a withdrawal rate based on today's factors. And, we don't mitigate the other risks in retirement. Eventually, due to inflation primarily, the withdrawals must invade principal. This starts a downward spiral of asset depletion, resulting in the client running out of money.

We have to challenge our thinking about income distribution and asset accumulation so that both counterbalance one another. Today, we use one to fund the other. But, they need to complement each other throughout a client's lifetime.

If you're using a simple withdrawal strategy for income, chances are the withdrawal rate will escalate in the client's late 70s and 80s. This adds pressure to the remaining portfolio and might eliminate options. Instead, think about designing a guaranteed, inflation-adjusted floor of income and creating liquidity with funds that don't supply income. At the same time, complement the plan with risk mitigation products to increase the probability for success.

Winning Strategy: You've heard the saying "It's not what you earn; it's what you keep that matters." Well, it's not the distribution rate when you start that matters; it's the rate in the second half of retirement that makes retirement sustainable.

Lessons Learned ... Again

September 2, 2015

In November 2014, I wrote about a short correction in the market. Over a period of 22 trading days in the fourth quarter of 2014, the market corrected and wiped out more than $1 trillion of wealth. Clients never really felt that loss, however, because it came and rebounded before the next quarterly statement. Once again, we're witnessing wild market swings with many clients concerned about their retirement savings. Their concerns are only fueled further by instant news and financial news outlets.

From August 17-24, 2015, we've seen global economic concerns impact the financial markets severely. During times of market volatility, it's important to remember the fundamentals of financial planning and to deliver on those fundamentals through the planning process. While no planning process fully insulates you from market fluctuations, long-standing principles used in previous volatile markets can provide insights – some that have worked and some that continue to be refined. I want to offer a refresher on some of these basic principles and add some insight from what we've learned works best in all markets.

Product allocation before asset allocation (i.e., focus on what's really important to each client): In the past, we've focused on building a portfolio based on negative correlations and asset classes that don't always move in the same direction. Math and science point to product allocation being just as important, if not more important. Not all products were built to accomplish the same purpose, so it's necessary to build a portfolio of products that meet the client's needs before we focus on asset allocation.

Start with securing income: When using a variety of products to solve client needs, you should discuss the need for a secure retirement income. A client exponentially enjoys their retirement when they're meeting their essential expenses and adding an inflation hedge. Secure income can come in many forms; however, planners must look at various sources that minimize the amount of capital needed to secure it. Essential expenses should be met with dependable income streams. The liquidity-free capital can be used for other goals and desires.

Mitigate longevity risks: Longevity is a multiplier for all risks in retirement. Statistically, the risks of asset allocation, health care costs, and long-term care costs grow when longevity is not addressed. Positioning the proper amount of assets in the proper vehicles to mitigate longevity allows a client to minimize all other risks to proper levels. Thus, the rest of the financial plan may be met with more reasonable assumptions and expectations.

Address legacy goals: Making sure other risks, like disability and death, are addressed creates security that the family's goals and objectives will be met in the short term and long term. A financial plan without these elements is doomed. More importantly, cash value life insurance can provide a resource to supplement retirement income during market volatility, which is when you least want to withdraw assets from your investments.

Evaluate tax efficiency and fee drag: When choosing financial solutions, it's important to consider the impact of taxation, especially on income-generating vehicles. It's not what you earn; it's what you keep. With the ever-changing and more complex financial solutions, many financial plans include expensive riders. As we enter a fiduciary role for all our transactions, fee drag and tax consequences must be considerations that we evaluate in our solutions.

Winning Strategy: Today, more than ever, Americans need strong financial advice. During times of financial extremes – both up and down – it's important to stay fundamentally strong. I challenge you to take a look at your financial plans. Evaluate how close you are to the fundamentals.

If you've strayed, my guess is that you have some anxious clients. If you've remained fundamentally strong through the six-year bull market, my guess is that you're earning your clients' trust during these volatile markets.

Generating Income
July 16, 2014

In today's current interest rate environment, have you ever wondered what it would take to generate $10,000 in annual income?

According to BankRate.com, the current (July 16, 2014) national averages on one-year and five-year CDs are .23 percent and .78 percent, respectively. The highest rates are 1.10 percent on a one-year CD and 2.30 percent on a five-year CD. The 10-year treasury is approximately 2.58 percent.

At those yields, this is what a lump-sum deposit would have to be to get $10,000 a year in annual income:

$$0.23\% = \$4,347,826$$
$$0.78\% = \$1,282,051$$
$$1.10\% = \$909,091$$
$$2.30\% = \$434,783$$
$$2.58\% = \$387,597$$

With an indexed annuity, executing the guaranteed income rider after one year, a 65-year-old client would only need a deposit of $166,800 to generate the same $10,000 a year in annual income.

Winning Strategy: With so many investment options, an indexed annuity with an income rider may be a good solution for your clients to help them overcome this low-interest-rate environment.

Income is Temporary
April 10, 2014

One of the most unique products for income planning is Temporary Life. This single-premium annuity provides an increased income stream when the client is willing to assume some of the longevity risks. If placed correctly, Temporary Life can increase payout and enhance the overall return associated with income planning.

If you wanted to generate $9,000 a month for a male, age 70, based on a life and 15-year certain payout, the client would need to purchase a $134,902.09 single-premium immediate annuity.* If the client utilized Temporary Life for 15 years, the premium needed is reduced to $100,861.92. Let's assume the difference ($34,040) is invested, and it earns a net 6 percent for the 15 years. That investment would grow to $81,579.24 by the end of the 15th year.

If the client had deposited the full $134,902, taken $9,000 annually and ended with $81,579 as an account balance, the gross return is 4.81 percent. More importantly, you would have to find an income rider generating a 6.67 percent payout to match the annual income.

In this case, Temporary Life has taken the client to near life expectancy with a substantially higher annual income. The unused premium creates a side fund to use for emergencies or for additional income at age 85.

Winning Strategy: It's easy to look at variable annuities with income riders for solutions, but there are alternatives that can provide clients more options, flexibility and better benefits.

Rates as of March 24, 2014, from A+ carrier with a 96 Comdex

Taking Retirement Across the Goal Line
March 10, 2014

Statistically, in the NFL, teams score the most points in the final two minutes of each half. It's called the two-minute drill. In order to be considered a great quarterback, you must precisely orchestrate those minutes in close games. Doing so is the difference between winning and losing many games. There seems to be less stress around the team when a quarterback runs the two-minute drill to perfection, and there is a clear path to late-game success.

In retirement planning, it's important to be the same type of quarterback or planner for our clients. The late-game heroics are what separate the trusted advisor from the everyday planner.

Clients obsess over how their later retirement years will look. It's not just the year the client runs out of money that is stressful; it's the years leading up to that point which force lifestyle changes and emotional pain within families. Clients need to know plans are in place to have a long, successful retirement.

Lifetime income products provide a level of certainty. Control and access are built into newly designed products. By positioning some products to begin income at life expectancy calculations, you can leverage a client's mortality credits and supply them with a higher income level during their own two-minute drills.

Winning Strategy: By creating confidence in the late game, advisors gain trust with clients. Rethinking conventional products in an unconventional manner proves to be the difference in many situations.

The Swinging Pendulum
May 15, 2014

Understanding client behavior has always been an interesting – if not challenging – aspect of the financial planning process for me. Sometimes it seems that clients move in opposite directions from what logic would dictate.

That said, client trends remain one of the most important pieces of knowledge we can possess when we meet with our clients and prospects.

A Towers Watson research paper released in May 2014 showed that consumer behavior has moved opposite of where we would typically think. Today, 62 percent of Americans would be willing to give up some current pay or salary for a guaranteed income stream in the future.* While most companies are looking to take pensions off the books because they don't help the recruiting process, the majority of Americans are looking for pension-like income. It appears we are not aligned with our clients.

The need for guaranteed income is a major shift from just five years ago. In the same survey in 2009, only 46 percent of Americans said they would give up some portion of their earnings to have guaranteed retirement income. Think about the time in which that survey was conducted – 2009. The financial crisis was fresh in everyone's mind, defined contribution account balances had fallen as much as 40 percent, and prospects were bleak for economic growth. Yet, as most account balances have nearly rebounded, more Americans want guaranteed income.

Clients can no longer expect guarantees from their employers. With the Pension Protection Act and proposed changes to Pension Benefit Guaranty Corporation premiums, it is unlikely that most employers will reinstate pension contributions.

Winning Strategy: As planners, we must provide guaranteed solutions to our clients. We need to set aside our egos relative to money management and realize that our clients want some level of base, guaranteed income.

*Towers Watson Global Benefits Attitude Survey, May 2014.

Three Overlooked Retirement Risks
June 12, 2014

The American College's Retirement Income Certified Professional (RICP)® curriculum includes a list of 27 risks that retirees face. Here are three risks that are incredibly important but often overlooked.

1. **Forced retirement:** Your client plans to work until age 66 in order to retire with full Social Security benefits. Unfortunately, a health, family or employment issue forces them to retire at 61. Are they financially prepared to support the lifestyle to which they've grown accustomed?

   This happens more often than you would think. According to a recent Gallup poll, the average American retirement age is 62.*

2. **Loss of spouse:** What happens to the family income upon the death of a spouse? It is imperative to evaluate

survivor benefits in pensions and Social Security.

What may feel like a comfortable retirement can become downright terrifying upon the death of a spouse. Income sources are often halved, yet lifestyle costs for the widow(er) remain very similar to those of a couple. The last thing they need to be concerned with is how to replace lost income after the death of their spouse.

3. **Legacy:** Retirement income planning is all about balance. Balancing competing interests is the name of the game.

Think of your financially successful clients and prospects who want to maximize both their retirement income and their legacy assets while minimizing market risk. For them, using income guarantees can result in a more efficient allocation for income (generating the highest guaranteed income with the least amount of assets), allowing the remaining assets to be managed to achieve their legacy goals.

Winning Strategy: If your clients don't have the benefit of a crystal ball, shifting these uncontrollable significant risks to an insurance solution is sound advice.

Gallup, "Average U.S. Retirement Age Rises to 62," April 28, 2014.

What's in a Rate of Return?

February 20, 2014

If we don't compare apples to oranges, then why do we compare rates of return equally? There are so many components to the real rate of return that people ignore them when they choose investment vehicles. If we look at the real return to clients, many vehicles look similar ... so why take on additional risk for similar returns?

Let's take Paul and John as an example. Paul likes the idea of investing in a group of sub-accounts in a variable annuity with an income rider to protect his income. John, on the other hand, wants to protect his income but does not want to risk principal; so, he places his retirement money into a fixed indexed annuity. Paul's investments average 7 percent per year, but he pays 1.25 percent for M&E; 1.35 percent for the cost of the rider; and 0.95 percent for the asset management fees on the sub-accounts. His real rate of return is 3.55 percent (7 percent - 1.25 percent - 1.35 percent - 0.95 percent).

John has an identical income rider with a guaranteed roll-up and income for life. His cap rate is 6 percent. During his holding period, the market hits the cap 80 percent of the time (statistical average) for an index gain of 4.8 percent. After the cost of the income rider (0.95 percent), John's retirement money grows at 3.85 percent without any downside returns due to the fixed indexed annuity.

Winning Strategy: The lure of unlimited upside potential comes at a cost in terms of fees and rider costs. It's important to have a discussion with clients about the real rate of return and not just the nominal return. Nominal returns are returns that sell, but the real return is what generates client growth. Said another way: It's not what you earn; it's what you keep.

Buying Income on Sale

January 7, 2016

Last Sunday, my wife asked me to go to the grocery store. She was studying and writing papers as she continues her education to become an ultrasound technician, so I agreed to shop if she provided me with a list. Having been recently married, it was different for me to buy more than hot dogs, Eggo waffles and bread. But I figured it out, and I found myself shopping the way most Americans do.

As I went methodically down the list, I wheeled my cart from aisle to aisle searching for each item. Once I found the paper towels, I looked at the brands and designs, then I made my decision. However, I found myself looking at the cost. It was clearly a better deal to purchase 12 rolls of paper towels instead of four. Without hesitation, I purchased the dozen – even though I didn't need all of them now and the total cost was more.

Next, I found the facial tissue and repeated the same decision process: brand, design, cost per box. I'm now the proud owner of a dozen boxes of Kleenex.

Here's my question: Why aren't we using the same process with our clients when it comes to retirement income? When you look at the options, the most efficient way to purchase income is to take advantage of discounted dollars and mortality credits. And, only one type of vehicle provides the advantage of mortality credits and tax-advantaged income distribution rules. Even though that purchase may be more in today's dollars, it will likely outperform many traditional vehicles that possess volatility, sequence of return risk, longevity risk, and gain-first taxation.

It's time to have a conversation about buying basics. If we're willing to pay more for a larger supply of paper towels and Kleenex because we know we'll need them later, there's no reason we shouldn't be doing the same with our income products. Most people are willing to spend a few extra dollars now to save more in the long run.

Ask your clients how they shop at the grocery store. If they're willing to purchase additional items when they're on sale, they're likely to be receptive to buying income at a discount as well.

Winning Strategy: Buying income at a discount is no different than buying basic necessities. And, our income floor is a necessity that should be guaranteed. Make sure you're showing your clients how they can buy in discounted dollars.

Part I

Retirement Income Strategies

Thoughts from Others

Annuities: Insured Income

By Steve Schankerman - August 3, 2015

In their lifetimes, your clients will own several kinds of insurance. For example, let's look at Jim, a 45-year-old man who's got a house, wife, two kids, a truck and a great job as an electrical engineer.

Like most people, Jim has health insurance through his employer to help cover his family's medical bills should they get sick or injured. He buys his home and auto insurance through his buddy Pete, a property a casualty agent in town. Pete also told Jim he should have life insurance to replace his income for his family should he pass away prematurely. So, he added that as well.

Jim's feeling pretty covered at this point. But he worries about the future. He hopes to retire in about 20 years, but he wants to make sure he'll have enough money to last – he doesn't want to run out of income later in life.

Well, in a few years, Jim could consider another type of insurance: an annuity. Just as life insurance offers a benefit for a shorter-than-expected life, an annuity can offer income for a longer-than-expected life.

An annuity is a long-term product designed for retirement income – it's a contract between a client and an insurance company. Jim, and other clients like him, can use a portion of their retirement fund to purchase a guaranteed stream of income, potentially for life.

An annuity could create reliable income for Jim, helping to fill the gap in his retirement income plan no matter how long he lives. Additionally, depending on the type of annuity he chooses, he may be able to access his contract value for long-term care needs should he need to, and/or a death benefit for his beneficiaries.

Winning Strategy: Annuities are an insurance product – they're insurance for your clients' retirement income.

Who's Benefiting from Annuities?

By John Duchien - February 2, 2015

Were your clients attracted to an annuity because of the ability to convert its value into a guaranteed stream of income – through annuitization or a lifetime income rider? The options are attractive, so it's likely you have a few clients who fit that bill.

Statistics show, however, that only a small percentage of clients take advantage of those features – less than 5 percent of annuities are ever converted into an income stream.* This means the vast majority of annuities will eventually pass to the owner's beneficiary upon their death.

Knowing those facts, you should talk to your clients about death benefit riders that are now available on select indexed annuities. Choosing a death benefit rider (available with a cost assessed at the end of each contract year and with NO medical underwriting) could allow your client's beneficiary to receive an enhanced roll-up value as a death benefit, all the while providing payout options and the opportunity to spread out their tax liability.

Winning Strategy: Instead of discussing interest rates and caps, talk to your clients about how death benefit riders on indexed annuities can create a legacy for their loved ones.

*LifeHealthPro,"Ruark study: Annuitization rates are below 5 percent," Jan. 30, 2013

Importance of a Guarantee

By Jeff Hood - February 5, 2015

How important is guaranteed income? Ask any retiree or near-retiree, or read most any survey about concerns in retirement, and the most common fear is running out of money. Financial planners must consider what assets are available and what tools they have available to create and generate guaranteed, lifetime income.

Today, one tool often used in financial plans is an annuity with an income rider. An income rider guarantees an income payment for the life of the insured, and can even be set up to guarantee income payments for the insured's spouse. Clients may even have the option for increasing income payments under some annuity contracts.

Here's how it works: The average payout factor at age 70 is 5 percent. If your income base amount is $200,000, then the resulting payout is $10,000. In most cases, this would be the amount the insured would be guaranteed on an annual basis for their lifetime.

With an increasing income payment option, when there is any interest credited to the annuity, the insurance company increases the last annual payment amount by the interest earned, expressed as a percentage. Say your annual income payment was $10,000; however in the last contract year, you earned 4 percent in interest. The insurance company would then increase your lifetime annual income payment to $10,400. Choosing this option would help you keep pace with inflation, and potentially help you offset higher health care and other costs.

Winning Strategy: Guaranteed lifetime income is important to many of your clients. Show them options with annuities and income riders.

Simple is as Simple Does

By Jim Martin - January 29, 2015

Sounds like a line from Forrest Gump, doesn't it? That may be the case, but the phrase also serves as an apt description for one of the major benefits of fixed annuities: simplicity. I've never heard a client complain because their portfolio or financial plan was "not complex enough." Have you?

Couple simplicity with tax deferral, liquidity, low to no fees, and guaranteed rates, principal and income, and you have a very desirable product for your conservative clients and those looking to build a solid foundation under a more aggressive portfolio.

Oh, and how about two more benefits that may be the most important of all, especially in today's economic environment? Correction protection and increasing future income.

A market correction is imminent – perhaps not this month or this year, but potentially next year or shortly after. Existing or soon-to-be-realized market gains are increasingly in jeopardy if they're not locked in soon. A fixed indexed annuity can protect those gains and give your clients the chance to participate in near-term gains, yet to be, before the correction.

Concerning income: If generating income now is important, will it be any less so in the future? No, it will be more critical in the future. Increasing income riders on fixed indexed annuities can guarantee future income increases for minimal cost compared to other alternatives.

Winning Strategy: Simplicity has value and is only one of the many benefits that fixed annuities provide. With a market correction on the horizon, staying in place and not going backwards is progress.

The Transition Phase

By Jason Caudill - July 24, 2014

Annuity sales typically fit into one of three categories: accumulation, distribution or wealth transfer. However, with the rise in the importance of retirement income planning and all of the income riders now available, there is another category: transition.

Individuals who are 5-10 years from retirement are usually considered to be in the transition phase. These clients have a few more years to invest for growth before they need to start their retirement income stream. Think about this hypothetical client:

- Age 60
- Starting retirement income at age 65
- Depositing $100,000 into an variable annuity

Assuming a 9.2 percent compound rate of return, in five years the variable annuity would be worth $155,000. At a 4.5 percent payout rate, it would generate a lifetime income of $7,000 annually.

Now, take the same client and invest his $100,000 in an indexed annuity with a lifetime income rider. This client could be better off because even in a Doomsday scenario, the indexed annuity should perform at least equal to the variable annuity, while keeping the charges much lower than traditional variable annuity fees and expenses.

Winning Strategy: With so many income rider options available on indexed annuities today, it can sometimes be a challenge to determine which rider is the best choice for your clients in transition. Take a look at all of their options for guaranteed retirement income.

How Income Riders Provide Guarantees and Flexibility
By Bentley Heese - December 11, 2014

Today's income riders available with fixed indexed annuities (FIAs) have evolved tremendously over the past several years, based on what clients want, as well as what they need. Ten years ago, clients had to turn to variable annuities if they wanted a compelling income rider, but insurance companies have heard clients' demands and have stepped up to deliver.

Clients want guarantees, flexibility, liquidity and control. Not every income rider or annuity has all four components, but you can customize an annuity plan based on your client's personal priorities.

Let's discuss guarantees, flexibility, liquidity and control. FIAs always have a guarantee on the downside, and now a rider may be added to guarantee that a client will never run out of income. These are not annuitized riders, they are guaranteed minimum withdrawal benefits. Yes, if the contract value does go to zero, there is no cash value left, but the income continues until death of the client(s).

This approach also gives the client much more flexibility in how they receive the income and take the withdrawals. The withdrawals may be stopped and started, and in some cases, the deferral will go back into the contract or be held in a separate "bucket" for future use. This may be useful from a tax liability standpoint if a client is close to moving into a higher bracket.

Because the withdrawals are not annuitized and the client can turn them on or off, this also gives them control. It enables them to maintain contract value for a longer period of time if the value does start to decline and they do not wish to take all of the income available. The degree of control varies between carriers – some allow the income to start immediately while some require at least a year of waiting and also restrict the client as to when they can turn on the rider (anniversary date only or daily roll-up).

All insurance companies reward clients who wait by offering roll-ups and/or age-based withdrawal factors. Find out when and how the client plans to use the rider, and you can find the best fit.

Most annuities have more-than-adequate liquidity provisions as well. With FIAs, it is generally 10 percent – this is either 10 percent of the premium or contract value. If it is the contract value, the client usually must wait a year. Some carriers even allow withdrawals without triggering the income rider.

The best recommendation I can make is to ask your client what they feel is most important. When do they want to start taking income? How much flexibility do they want with those withdrawals?

Winning Strategy: Know your clients and their hot buttons – drill down and find the best match for them. It may even make sense to split your client's funds between two carriers, based on what they are trying to achieve.

Insure to Be Sure

By Jeff Hood - May 14, 2014

According to a recent MarketWatch survey, 52 percent of retirees said they are pulling money out of their retirement accounts simply as the need arises – with no real plan in place.* Most retirees fail to create an income plan, yet poll after poll suggests that their biggest worry is outliving their money.

So what advice are these retirees given?

- Stick to a budget
- Cut expenses
- Make sure you have the right mix of stocks and bonds in your retirement accounts

The list of advice goes on and on ....

I say if you want to BE sure ... INSURE. Consider an annuity with a lifetime income rider. This strategy GUARANTEES a lifetime income payment for as long as you live.

A client's lifetime income payment is based on their annuity income base and their age when they decide to start lifetime income payments. Some annuities even offer an increasing lifetime payment opportunity. Most importantly, employing this strategy guarantees an income payment for life.

Winning Strategy: It is worth repeating: If you want to BE sure ... INSURE!

MarketWatch, "Most Retirees Fail to Have an Income Plan," May 6, 2014.

Increasing Income in Retirement

By Randy Kitzmiller - July 8, 2014

If your clients want to maintain their standard of living throughout retirement, they need increasing income as part of their strategy.

Take for example a couple, both age 65. It's likely that one of them will live an additional 24 years. If you use the Rule of 72 (years required to double investment = 72 ÷ compound annual interest rate) at a 3 percent inflation rate, they will need to DOUBLE their income in those 24 years to keep up with the same standard of living.

The math doesn't quite add up with a variable annuity with a high water mark strategy. If they have an income value of $1 million and a 5 percent payout, they start with $50,000 of income. For their income to increase to $100,000 in 24 years, they need the income value to grow to $2 million. While mathematically this sounds possible, don't forget that they have to overcome a 5 percent withdrawal, fees of up to 3.5 percent and any market loss.

Using an annuity income strategy gives you much better odds. Your clients will get an annual reset in the income and accumulation phase, and approximately 77 percent of the time, they would receive an increase in income.

Winning Strategy: Don't wait 24 years to find out if your clients have enough income. Increase their odds and income by looking at different annuity strategies today.

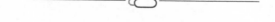

Using the 'Happily Ever After' Close

By Jim Martin - November 17, 2014

I've noticed many times that the difference between an A-level advisor and an A-plus advisor may come down to one simple factor: An A-level advisor gets their client to retirement; an A-plus advisor gets their client to and through retirement!

Being an A-level advisor is like reading a novel about an incredible journey, then stopping when the travelers get to their destination. An A-plus advisor keeps reading – they want to know what happens to the travelers after they've arrived. If you're selling multi-year guarantee annuities (MYGAs) or fixed index annuities (FIAs) with no income riders, you may not be providing your clients with the best ending to their retirement journey story.

While your clients will do better with MYGA rates than they will with bank products, FIAs will historically perform better. If you're using FIAs already, great! But consider this: At the end of the surrender charge period, what will your clients' worlds look like? In five to seven years, will they be less or more conservative? How will market performance over that period (i.e., the inevitable market correction) impact their attitudes?

Five to seven years from now, your clients will be older and closer to or in retirement. Couple that with having gone through a likely market correction, and there's a good possibility they'll be more conservative. Most clients assuredly will be more concerned with locking in some degree of retirement income.

So, where am I going with this?

A select group of FIA income riders are available to increase your clients' payout percentages the longer they hold the contract before taking income. So by buying the rider now, they can lock in payout percentages that are guaranteed to increase.

For example, a 60-year-old who purchases a rider today could get a guaranteed payout percentage of 7 percent in five years (9 percent in 10 years). If that same 60-year-old waits five years to try and find an income rider, their payout percentage would be around 5 percent (5.5 percent in 10 years), based on current products available.

With higher guaranteed payout percentages purchased today, there's less pressure on earnings (market correction protection) and greater potential retirement income for clients who will soon be older and possibly more conservative.

Winning Strategy: Purchasing an FIA with an income rider might just provide your clients the "happily ever after" ending they were hoping for.

Retirement Income Opportunity Ready to Explode

By Ryan McGee - September 25, 2014

Today, the United States has 42 million retirees, and by 2025, the number will grow to 65 million – meaning nearly 4 million people a year will be entering retirement.[1] LIMRA estimates that the value of assets held by those ages 55 and above will double to nearly 22 trillion by 2020.[2]

This opportunity was validated by a 2013 BlackRock Investor Pulse Survey.[3] Key takeaways from the polled investors (defined as having investable assets of $50,000 or more) include:

- 62% were concerned about having enough income from investments to live comfortably in retirement
- 54% agreed with the statement "I'm worried about outliving my savings"
- 73% agreed, "Keeping my money safe is more important to me than trying to generate returns"

BlackRock President Rob Kapito said, "People are living longer than ever before, dramatically altering the financial challenges of retirement ... Increased longevity is a blessing, but it's an expensive one because that translates into the need for a bigger retirement nest egg and access to secure, retirement-long income. As our survey suggests, many Americans simply won't have the money they need to enjoy their longer lives if they don't start investing differently."

Winning Strategy: If you aren't educating yourself on guaranteed income options for your clients, I'll bet they'll be asking another advisor instead.

[1]LIMRA, "LIMRA Secure Retirement Institute: Total Annuity Sales Grow 17 Percent in Fourth Quarter," Feb. 24, 2014.
[2]LIMRA "LIMRA Predicts Retirement Income Opportunity Reaches $22 Trillion by 2020," Feb. 4, 2013.
[3]BlackRock Investor Pulse Survey, 2013.

IRS Greenlights New Roth IRA Rollover Regulations
By Bill Stutz - September 22, 2014

Last week, the Internal Revenue Service provided guidance that permits employees to roll over their after-tax contributions directly into a Roth IRA, tax-free. This ruling applies to rollovers from 401(k),

403(b) or 457 plans.

You can read Notice 2014-54 "Guidance on Allocation of After-Tax Amounts to Rollovers" at http://www.irs.gov/pub/irs-drop/n-14-54.pdf

The notice states: "The applicability date of the regulations is proposed to be Jan. 1, 2015. However, in accordance with § 7805(b)(7), taxpayers are permitted to apply the proposed regulations to distributions made before the applicability date, so long as such earlier distributions are made on or after Sept. 18, 2014."

Here's an example of how it would work:

- Retirement plan account value: $200,000
- Pre-tax amount: $150,000
- After-tax amount: $50,000
- Total distribution: $200,000
- Tax-free rollover to traditional IRA: $150,000
- Convert tax-free to Roth IRA: $50,000

Opportunities

1. Check in with clients to determine if they have after-tax money in their retirement plans and, if not, see if they can make such contributions. Not all plans are created equal – you will need to check the plan document for rules on after-tax contributions.

2. Your clients can benefit from tax-deferred savings on money that's already been subject to income taxes and then convert it to a Roth IRA upon distribution. This will generally apply to higher income clients who can afford the larger contributions, but because of their income they are likely ineligible to make annual contributions to a Roth.

3. Clients over age 59 ½ with after-tax contributions in their retirement plans can take advantage of non-hardship in-service withdrawals and roll both pre- and post-tax contributions into traditional and Roth IRAs.

Winning Strategy: Last but not least …. What's better than tax-free retirement income? Tax-free retirement income guaranteed for life! If your client or prospect's Roth IRA will be a source of retirement income (as opposed to a way to pass this wealth tax-free to children or grandchildren), doesn't it make sense that this income should last as long as the client and their spouse live? An annuity may be the answer.

Take Client Gains off the Table

By Dan Lavigne - May 30, 2014

How many of your clients have asked if you think this market is due for a correction? Who is more concerned about it – your clients or you? I'm not saying that the party is over on Wall Street, but I do know the bears haven't eaten in a long time.

My point is this: Every day that we let go by without taking some part of our clients' gains off the table, the greater we are multiplying their risk. Yes, multiplying! Adding risk occurs when we change their asset allocation to a more aggressive mix. Multiplying risk occurs when we stack or compound risk factors, such as a market that hasn't retraced gains in nearly five years with P/Es nearing the range of the 1987 crash, coupled to an economy with the lowest employment rate in 39 years and a bond market that mirrors Japan's 20 years ago.

I'm sure some of you will accuse me of fear-mongering. That's what those fixed indexed annuity guys do, right? Except I also wholesale three variable annuities and a mutual fund family, and I have a Series 24.

Winning Strategy: So how do I suggest we proceed? I thought you'd never ask! Look at all your options, including annuities, to help your clients avoid being bitten by the hungry bears.

Part II

Sales Motivation

Thoughts from Mike

Tools I Didn't Know Existed

June 11, 2015

One of our carrier partners visited a couple of weeks ago, and I talked to the wholesaler about her friend who is an ultra-marathoner, running more than 100 miles in races. We also talked about my running, which had been reduced because of some hip pain I began experiencing. At that point, I was only able to run one or two miles before my hip hurt so much I had to stop running.

The wholesaler mentioned a shoe I'd never heard of before – the Hoka One One. She had me look it up right away, and at first glance, I thought it looked like a heavy brick you would attach to your feet. She talked about the cushion and explained that her friend was able to complete long runs comfortably since moving to this shoe. I remained skeptical. I'd been loyal to the same brand and same shoe for the past seven years of running. Every other time I tried a new shoe, I got blisters, foot pain and hip pain, so I always ended back in the same model as before.

Reluctantly, I decided I had to try something to help my hip, and there was specialty running store where I was going to be staying for the weekend. I purchased the Hokas – they were the most expensive running shoes I had ever purchased. However, they are incredibility comfortable. In the prior 30 days, I had only been able to run about 20 miles total due to the pain. In the first week of wearing the Hokas,

I've been able to run 11 miles comfortably. I'm back to increasing my mileage, improving my times and enjoying my running.

I share this experience as an example of, "You don't know what you don't know." I was locked into one shoe because I had success with it previously. But, my body has changed – as do economic environments, client expectations, client goals and purposes of monies.

We have to be more open to looking at alternatives. Even slight adjustments or updates can greatly enhance our chances for success. Instead of thinking about your old, comfortable shoes, try to think about how the new, improved, better chance for success shoe could help you. I challenge everyone to change their mindset, be open to new ideas to help clients, and be focused on finding solutions instead of remaining in their comfort zone.

Winning Strategy: We get comfortable with the way we do business. Challenge yourself to think differently, act differently and create different results with clients using different strategies.

--------------------⌒◯⌒--------------------

How Much Can Our Clients Lose?
April 23, 2015

Many planners I talk with say they educate their clients on a relative percentage basis. For example, they tell them bear markets are defined as 20 percent decreases. This approach may help clients grasp the concept, but it fails to take into consideration how much of their hard-earned money could be lost or how much their retirement assets are truly at risk today, versus previous corrections. Additionally, the client may not realize how that loss could affect their retirement income level.

If our clients realized how much more is at risk today than in 1987 or 2008, I feel they may consider being more conservative with some of their assets. Instead, we hide behind the fact that recent corrections have lasted only "x" number of months or have been only "y" percent in depth. What does it mean to the client? Potentially, a lot of dollars.

In the crash of 1987, the stock market lost approximately $500 billion of market capitalization in one day. That represented a 22.6

percent downturn in the market indices.[1] Today, the S&P 500 retains a market capitalization of $19.7 trillion.[2] If the same correction/crash would occur, investors would lose $4.45 trillion dollars – nearly nine times the wealth.

We have a responsibility to protect wealth for our clients – not just grow it. To look at it differently, one of the best strategies to growth wealth is to take away some of the decreases that might happen along the way. There are vehicles designed to assist clients in this regard. In the correction of October 2014, investors lost $1.3 trillion of wealth. However, I've always argued most consumers didn't even feel or see that dip because it happened between statement cycles. (The S&P 500 only lost 1 point between quarterly statements the client would have received.)

When you talk to clients, I'd like you to discuss the real economic value of a correction – in hard dollars. Clients need the transparency of knowing exactly how a percentage change equates to their retirement and potential losses.

Winning Strategy: Don't hide behind percentages and historical data. Talk real dollars. Clients deserve to know how changes could impact their assets and future retirement income.

[1] *The Bubble Bubble, "Black Monday – the Stock Market Crash of 1987," Aug. 3, 2012.*
[2] *S&P Dow Jones Indices, Equity, S&P 500 Fact Sheet, Feb. 27, 2015.*

Things Will Change

July 2, 2015

I just left a well-attended broker-dealer roundtable, where the crowd was the largest in the semi-annual meeting's history. The content was the likely reason – the meeting focused on the U.S. Department of Labor's (DOL's) proposed fiduciary standards.

The DOL's proposal creates many obstacles for registered representatives. The fiduciary standard reaches many aspects of financial planning involving insurance and investment products.

Past rules protecting the state regulation of insurance products are circumvented through tougher language focused on impartial and unbiased recommendations to the client.

While no one wants less than a best-interest-of-the-client philosophy in our industry, policing the standards and implementing consequences would be far reaching. Additional disclosures, reductions in revenues, likely minimum account balances, and retooling of existing products to meet mandates (and not consumer interests) may be required if the proposal is accepted in its current form.

Clearly, as I have said many times in this blog, it's time for our industry to change – to better itself – by developing innovative products, gaining a deeper understanding of our clients and securing income through more options.

But, the end result of this proposal will be to eliminate the willingness of financial firms and their advisors to address the needs of middle Americans. This group needs professional advice more than any group in America right now. According to the American College's Retirement Income Certified Professional© program, 70 percent of middle Americans' wealth is tied up in non-financial assets. That means the amount of financial wealth this group has must be used wisely and efficiently for the highest priority needs – guaranteed expense coverage. We must look at the best possible use of dollars and attempt to secure the best possible lifestyle and legacy. That's their best interest.

Additional paperwork doesn't promise the best interests of the client. More importantly, leaving the policing of the fiduciary standard to litigation opens a door of responsibility that most firms will be unwilling to take in the future. I challenge all our advisors to pay close attention to these proposed regulations and changes in procedures over the next 18 months. Be active in your professional organizations and local government bodies to voice your opinion. It might be the best practice management time you spend to protect your financial firm.

Winning Strategy: Our business is about to change. Can we stop the onerous regulation and have meaningful and impactful change to our clients?

A One-Man Wrecking Crew
June 18, 2015

If you followed the 2015 NBA Finals, you know the Cleveland Cavaliers lost two of their five starters late in the season and in the playoffs. Regardless, the team made it to game six of the finals before giving up the championship to the Golden State Warriors, who have the league's MVP, Stephen Curry. Maybe the best all-around player is LeBron James, who carried his injured Cavaliers team through the end of the season.

Everyone was cheering for the underdog team from Cleveland in hopes that LeBron could single-handedly win the series for the city. But while everyone was talking about how he's a one-man wrecking crew, they were also talking about his stamina, or rather lack thereof. One of the greatest athletes in the league, he appeared to be tired and run down in the playoffs. You can't blame him. He was forced to score more points, grab more rebounds and assist in more baskets than his teammates.

I think the Cavaliers demonstrated why a collaborative team approach is best – in basketball and financial planning. With Kevin Love and Kyrie Irving on the sideline, LeBron was forced to essentially do everything to fill the gap they left. While he made it work during this series, it clearly took a physical toll.

The same would be true for your financial planning practice. Too often, I see planners attempting to be the LeBron James of financial services. They try to do too much. In the end, they get tired, lose focus and makes errors. Their client base grows too large and the personal contact their clients loved quickly evaporates.

The solution? Make sure you build a team infrastructure into your planning process. If the primary relationship manager (you) isn't available, then envelope your clients with the bench strength they deserve (your team).

By building a team with a strong supporting cast, you can build a sustainable, profitable business model that your clients will appreciate.

While you might have short-term success (one playoff series) with just one superstar, long-term success (a championship) with a team approach creates value in your business and makes it referable.

Winning Strategy: Being the superstar might work in the short run, but having a strong bench adds value to your client relationships, which translate into wins for you.

What Fiduciary Should Mean to You
April 2, 2015

As the NCAA tournament unfolds, many people have been asking me about my experience at Indiana University during the basketball team's run to the 1987 national championship. Frequently, I get asked how it felt to be on the bench as a student manager during a game played in front of 70,000-plus people. Was it easy to stay focused on the game? How did the players maintain their poise? And, the pressure must have been intense, right?

Well, I'll tell you. When you are "in the moment," all the distractions seem to vanish or become far away from your focus. Even 70,000 people at high decibels won't faze a high level athlete. You tend to be focused on the task at hand and the execution of the game plan in order to succeed.

At the end of the day, that's the same philosophy we need to have when it comes to our clients. If we are solely focused on our clients, we will not be distracted by factors that cause us to stray from our mission: securing their finances.

The discussions around the fiduciary standards heats up and cools down. However, if we are truly "in the moment" with our clients, we have nothing to fear. It's when we focus on our business model that we become incongruent with our clients' needs and objectives. As financial professionals, staying focused on our clients and aligning our recommendations with them in mind keeps us within the fiduciary standard. Fiduciary is not a business model, but a way of doing business.

I encourage financial professionals to not be afraid of the fiduciary standard, but embrace it. If we really are acting in the best interests of our clients, we won't see a day-to-day change in the way we do business. It's important for our broker-dealers and institutions to understand the proposed standards don't require us to do business differently. True professionals, successful professionals, already conduct themselves in this manner.

Winning Strategy: Fiduciary is not a business model. It's a level of conduct where we focus on our client. Many of us are already there.

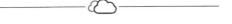

Baseballs and Tomatoes
April 9, 2015

Recently, I heard a great story about a man coaching his 7-year-old's baseball team. At practice, he was pitching to all the kids, and each would step up to the plate with their bat to take a few swings. As many kids tend to do, they'd stop their swing the moment the bat made contact with the ball. The result was more of a bunt than a hit – the ball would almost fall off the bat and trickle on the ground for a couple of feet. This would happen batter after batter. The coach tried to get his players to swing harder, get the bat in a better position, step into their swing, etc. Nothing changed.

Since his players couldn't seem to grasp what he was trying to teach them, the coach changed his own technique. He took the baseball in his hand and asked the batter what he was holding. The child looked at him as if it was a trick question. "It's a baseball, coach," the young boy said.

The coach said, "No, it's a tomato. I want you to think of this as a tomato and smash it!" The next pitch came, and the batter took the "home run swing" that the coach was looking for. From then on, each batter got up to the plate and swung so hard they nearly turned themselves around. But, they made good contact and got the ball out of the infield.

The players' success had nothing to do with their technique – it was about their mindset. The coach changed the way the batters thought of the ball. Instead of thinking of it as a hard object, each boy began thinking of a lighter, more fragile object he could easily bust up. Once their mindset was changed, success followed quickly.

I bring up this story for two reasons: First, baseball season is back in full swing (pun intended). Second, it reminded me of the problems many of us have when talking to our clients about their future. How often do we discuss rate of return, fees, style drift and other financial terms that are likely over their heads? Not that those things aren't important, but we have to focus on the clients' needs and how we can help address them.

We have to make it easier for our clients to understand the risks of living too long. It's time to ask questions about how they're going to live if they run out of money or need long-term care. More importantly, we have to change our story about how we can help them mitigate those risks. It starts with changing our own mindset ... then changing the conversation.

Winning Strategy: Think of positioning your clients' needs in a new light. If you can change their mindset about the problem, you're more likely to find a successful solution.

Winning with New Regulations
September 24, 2015

The proposed rule from the U.S. Department of Labor (DOL) takes up a lot of conversation these days. While we await the final rule, it's clear that we are likely to be acting in a fiduciary role soon. Many have predicted lower sales and as much as 25 percent of the sales force shrinking. However, with any change, there is opportunity to capture additional market share – even with increased regulation.

A large advice gap exists in the United Kingdom, where similar legislation went into effect in 2012. Many financial institutions moved up market as they did not find the mass affluent market profitable. Unlike advisors in the U.K., we will still be able to write commission-based products. Let's not lose sight of that fact in the conversations surrounding the DOL. For those financial professionals who can work efficiently in the mass affluent, there will likely be opportunity to thrive in the post-DOL world.

It will take efficiency and effectiveness – two business building blocks – in order to succeed in this market with the proposed regulations. Professionals earning a commission must be able to repeat a sales process with every client to assure the planning remains holistic. In order to capitalize on the opportunity that involves key components in the proposed rule, in 2015-16, you must think about strategic maneuvering:

- What level of staffing will help me in the post-DOL era?
- How can I easily document all of my client interactions, client conversations, client goals, and case-specific data that leads to my recommendations?
- What software will I need to show I am working in the best interest of my client while remaining carrier/fund/investment agnostic?
- How can I repeat the sales process efficiently, and with care, to create scale in my office?

Winning Strategy: New regulation does not mean you automatically have to change your business plan to a fee-based or assets under management model. However, it will require some thought about how to take advantage of some of the opportunities. I urge everyone to begin the thought process around a post-DOL conflict-of-interest era. The plans you make today are likely to help you and your clients succeed in the future.

How Will You Be Remembered?
September 3, 2015

I love good sports stories and analogies, as well as strange facts and figures from the sports world. So of course I enjoyed an article from USA Today Sports that listed 101 little-known sports facts.* One that jumped out at me? Bill Buckner has more hits than Ted Williams. Unfortunately, most people remember Bill Buckner for one error than they do for all his achievements at the plate.

This made me think about our business and our relationships, not only our clients, but also their beneficiaries. Do you want to be remembered for the one error you might have committed in the planning process? Or, will you be remembered for all the great years of returns you provided your client during their working years? You can accumulate a lot of money for your clients over their earning years, but if you fail to plan for their lifetime income, your legacy to their family will be dramatically different.

Watching their parents, kids see firsthand what their retirement lifestyle could be with you as an advisor. With a flawed history, your chances of managing the next generation's assets become slim to zero. If you haven't addressed their parents' longevity or health care concerns, they likely won't want to have the same experience. If you haven't taken care of their parents, why would they want you to take care of them?

At the end of the day, we can manage assets and build wealth all day long. We can out-gain the money manager across the street or beat the market indexes. But, if we commit an error in not addressing predictable, guaranteed, inflation-adjusted income for our clients, we will be remembered for our one error versus all the years of outperforming the market.

Winning Strategy: Don't let one error define your legacy for generations to come.

USA Today, *"101 incredible sports facts that will blow your mind,"* April 23, 2015.

Making for Meaningful Change
July 9, 2015

By now, many of you have heard about the U.S. Department of Labor's (DOL's) Fiduciary Standards. This will be a topic of much discussion in the coming weeks, months and, quite possibly, years to come. First, let me be clear I support the need for industry change that supports meaningful, constructive and enforceable standards in the best interests of our clients. We have a responsibility to keep their best interests in mind.

Getting to a point where we can keep our clients' best interests in mind and do so for all our clients is the challenge. In my opinion, the current version of the DOL's Fiduciary Standard is not the path to the best interests of clients across America. Today, we have too much emphasis on greed and equity growth with little focus on safe, guaranteed, dependable income through retirement – something many Americans desperately need. Unfortunately, there's almost no focus on utilizing non-financial wealth and diversifying income streams.

In June, I spent three days in Washington, D.C., talking to congressional leaders from my state and region about this problem as our industry continues to get its arms around the broad, sweeping impact of this proposal. As one speaker said this week, this will be the most significant regulatory overhaul in decades. If so, we have to get it right.

Workable solutions include:

- Crafting a "seller's exception" to allow certain transactions without triggering various fiduciary requirements so long as the consumer is clear that the agent is not providing investment advice and not acting as a fiduciary
- Maintain the 84-24 Prohibited Transaction Exception (PTE) for those products that are used in a transaction environment, not a fiduciary environment
- Draft a proposal that wouldn't restrict product choice, retaining affordability while creating access to retirement professionals for all Americans, not just those with larger balances that justify the risk of bringing them as a client

Overall, there remains a lot of work to be done on this initiative. The industry represents many independent, registered representatives and existing fiduciaries who secure the financial futures of many Americans. This decision creates a lot of risk for many – we must focus on meaningful change.

Change needs to take place, but it must make sense for our end-users, our clients, who trust us regardless of our business model. As I've said before, the fiduciary standard is a way of business; it's not a business model.

Winning Strategy: Our industry will definitely change in the next 18 months. We need to make sure the change is positive for our clients.

Winning Teams Have Infrastructure
May 28, 2015

At the end of the 2014 NFL season, I remember listening to a sports broadcast discussing the similarities of the four franchises in the conference championships. All these teams had something in common: infrastructure. It's an important ingredient for success in sports AND business.

The host pointed out that each team had built a championship contender through various methods: free agency, the draft, retaining talent through long-term contracts or some key trades. Two teams had MVP quarterbacks. Two other teams had rising quarterbacks. Some teams relied on the run more than others, and a couple relied heavily on the short passing game. The methods were different, but all led them to winning.

If you're going to succeed in business, you need to find a way to build (or partner with someone who has) infrastructure around you. In the financial services industry, you need to have:

- **People who can support your sales efforts** – Product specialists are key to positioning the correct solution with the right client situation.
- **Post-sales support** – You need to be able to get your pending business through the pipeline efficiently, with little need to touch paper after the client signs. You need to be able to focus on the next client solution.
- **Marketing** – You must have a team that understands our business, your business, your clients' needs, and how to brand that story repeatedly.
- **Cutting-edge resources** – Your staff needs to supply a flow of ideas and clients to you so that you are always looking for ways

to drive revenue through your office. A good brokerage agency can provide ideas through data-mining and understanding the coming trends in the industry.

- **Financial reporting** – Just like you ask of your clients, you must be able to understand where you earn your revenue and where you spend it. Make sure you are getting all the commission reporting from your carriers to make your life easier. Establish processes so you can monitor the financial health of your business.

If you don't have the resources to reinvest in your business today, then you should partner with organizations that can help with the above areas. You might find that their partnership is more valuable than having a single person on staff, and it may be more profitable to outsource many of the infrastructure needs listed above.

Winning Strategy: Successful teams and businesses have outstanding infrastructures surrounding them. Great producers focus on activities that solve client problems, while others handle the non-revenue activities.

Wishing You Were Better

July 23, 2015

Think back 10 years ago. Did you have competition in 2005? Did you think there were a lot of regulations prior to the financial crisis? Did you think it was difficult to do business back then? How would your answers change now? A lot is different, but at the end of the day, nothing has really changed.

Compared to a decade ago, there's more competition today, from a variety of channels. Banks are more prevalent in our industry. And, disruptors like Google are entering the business, making it easier to sell, underwrite, apply for and sell insurance. The financial services industry continues to evolve and, in general, grow in complexity. Because of that, more regulation burdens us than ever before.

Additionally, applications are longer, more information is

requested of clients, and our revenues continue to shrink. Nothing has really changed.

Jim Rohn, American author and businessperson, said to not waste time wishing things were different. Instead, you should wish you were better. One of my wholesalers told me our new world is difficult and challenging. I argue that today is just as challenging as it was 10 years ago, proportionally.

The successful salesperson will adapt. The successful salesperson will understand the new complexities of our industry. The successful salesperson will be more transparent than ever before and demonstrate the value he or she brings to the client engagement for the fee charged. At the end of the day, the successful advisor will simply get better.

This year, let's turn our attention to our skill sets. Focus on adapting to the changing environment by gaining new insights that will enhance the client relationship. Focus on becoming more effective at designing income-generating portfolios that provide guarantees, safety and predictable increases in income. Don't wish things were different (because they can never be the same); wish you were better – and do something about it!

Winning Strategy: Don't wish things would change back to, "The good ol' days." Wish you were better and focus on how you can improve for your clients' sake.

Working with Skill, Not Luck
October 22, 2015

"Shallow men believe in luck. Strong men believe in cause and effect."
– Ralph Waldo Emerson

Too often we tell a client things like, "I feel confident this strategy will work for you" or "Based on historical performance, this will work." What we're really saying is we're relying on luck. We hope the vehicles we've chosen perform exactly as they have in the past to provide the needed income. And, we assume the strategy won't need to be changed, adjusted or enhanced. "Set it and forget it" is a recipe for disaster.

As we look to the future with a fiduciary landscape in mind, I think it's important to make sure we're operating from a point of skill and not luck. Skill requires a greater understanding of the cause and effect of financial vehicles. Just understanding how a product works is no longer acceptable. We have to move to understanding how that particular product benefits the client in the best possible way.

The industry and its regulators continue to move toward science and away from art. In the near future, it will be imperative to substantiate your recommendations with certainty that they meet the best interests of your client. No longer can we rely on the art of selling, which is valued individually. Instead, our skills used to create that art need to rise to the top and not only be seen, but documented.

Winning Strategy: This is a change of mindset we must become used to if we are to survive as financial professionals. Being held to a higher standard isn't a bad thing or unsurmountable. It simply means we must operate our businesses differently while accomplishing the same client objectives. It's skill, not luck that will make a difference for so many Americans going forward.

Anticipating a Botched Punt

October 29, 2015

If you didn't watch it, there's a good chance you heard about it. When rivals Michigan and Michigan State met up in October, the Spartans capitalized on a fumbled punt attempt and grabbed a last-second touchdown to win the game. I listened to the final minutes on the radio while driving to dinner with my wife – the announcers were nearly speechless. In the aftermath of that wild finish, I've heard superlatives like "unthinkable," "improbable," "given away" or "unbelievable." I even read a statistic that indicated Michigan State had a 0.2 percent chance of winning before the final play of the game.

As I think about that game in relation to my profession, two things keep going through my mind. First, it's important to finish strong. And second, it's important to plan for contingencies.

So many analogies can be made between retirement planning and the botched punt. In the final stages of life, the fear and anxiety of "not messing up" increase and create more pressure. This is no different than running out of money before you die or having the game rest in your hands. The anxiety that comes from a close game is no different than looking out five years and knowing you won't have enough money to last if you stay alive. The emotional struggles for immediate family and the next generation cannot be put into words.

Botched punt aside, we've seen several last-play wins this year in the Big Ten. I'm guessing the coaching staff didn't run through the possibility of something going wrong, preparing their teams for adverse situations … but you simply can't plan for every possibility.

However, in retirement planning, you can mitigate a lot of the risks that come at the end of the game. One risk is longevity and long-term care. You never know when or if a care event will happen to your clients during retirement, but you can take action today and reduce their risk – just like a coach running through contingency plans. By having the proper liquidity and funding for care events, your clients and their families can better react to unforeseen events. And, by planning for a long income stream, you can reduce everyone's anxiety.

Winning Strategy: Have you discussed or expected any "botched punts" in your clients' retirement plans? If not, you might be wise to plan for contingencies and talk to them about what to do in the event of living too long.

Change vs. Virtuosity
May 21, 2015

The definition of change is to convert or transform. Essentially, we all change year after year as we continue to transform as humans. But real, meaningful change might be better described as virtuosity – the development of great skill or mastery. So, what does it take to become virtuoso?

Becoming a virtuoso starts with one question: Am I resolved to be the best? If you are resolved to be a virtuoso, you have a purpose or intent to be the best. In doing so, you will do the things necessary to become the best – regardless of time commitments, money or effort. That is a clear difference to just changing.

As an industry, we have to be resolved to improve the client experience with underwriting, application processing and overall experience. We must commit to making the industry better, and do so in a manner that deploys financial resources, intellectual capital and time commitments from all levels.

We have to change our mindset from just change – because we are changing for the sake of change – to being resolved to make our industry a virtuoso industry. It has to be one that new talent views as a premier place to build a career, where clients seek information and don't rely on "robo-investing," and where we deliver true value to clients.

Winning Strategy: Re-think change to become a virtuoso and remember, the first step is redirecting our mindset.

Partnering to Differentiate
July 16, 2015

Many advisors are beginning to look alike, according to a recent article in OnWallStreet.com.*All of us are calling ourselves financial planners, wealth managers and asset managers. But our clients can't tell the difference because we essentially do all the same thing: grow assets.

One of the ways clients appear to be looking to differentiate financial advisors is through branding and digital marketing. As a business owner, you probably find it difficult to devote resources to things that don't directly generate revenue. However, our clients are looking for ancillary pieces of information to set us apart from the crowd. You need to make sure you're delivering educational information, specific client data and thought leadership through a variety of different mediums.

A lot of clients like shorter videos, for example. You can be concise while communicating complex ideas. Additionally, you need to think about how you can have a digital presence. This goes beyond just having a website. Fifteen years ago, having a simple website was innovative. Today, it's not only a table stake, but it's often viewed as old fashioned. Your clients will ultimately demand immediate access to their account values, beneficiary information and other key account data.

Gaining expertise on the latest technology remains expensive and time consuming. You need to have partners who can help you differentiate your business. It's no longer acceptable to be different because you're independent or take a holistic look at the client's situation. Instead, you have to do all of the above, plus deliver it when the client wants it – regardless of when they want it.

Take a look at your partnerships. Can they assist you with advancing in the digital world? Can they provide expertise in social media marketing, application design and promoting your business through referrals? If not, question why that person is considered a partner and insist on having the right partners by your side.

Winning Strategy: Partnerships are key to growth. Clients are looking for a different level of engagement with their financial professional. Make sure your partners are in line with where you need to go.

*On WallStreet, "Clients Say Firms Fail to Stand Out," June 15, 2015.

Why Financial Illiteracy is Like a Cancer
June 4, 2015

Recently, I read an article from Yahoo Sports about former Indiana Pacers player David Harrison.* After earning $4.4 million in four seasons with the NBA, plus some time overseas playing professionally, the 32-year-old basketball player is nearly broke. We've heard about these scenarios before, but this story exemplifies why financial illiteracy is like a cancer. It does not discriminate by wealth. It does not care about race or gender. Simply put, not understanding your financial situation and circumstances can ruin your life.

Harrison can't even work at a local McDonald's restaurant, not for lack of trying. Customers recognized him – it's difficult to miss a 7-foot person taking your order – causing them to ask questions and end up taking 40 minutes to order, according to the article. So he had to leave McDonald's. Banks foreclosed on his home and tried to repossess his car, and he still provides for his infant son. He says he can't even afford to finish the final 16 credit hours needed to earn a degree (he left college early to play in the NBA). Needless to say, his life now is extremely different from his life when he was playing in the NBA.

Even though most of us won't be retiring from the NBA, this example shows the importance of having a reliable stream of income when your main source of income stops – no matter your age or profession. It's something that's all-too-often overlooked. I'm sure Harrison would appreciate having some level of steady income right now. And, he probably wouldn't care about the rate of return on that income – he would be more focused on the bills he could pay instead.

Winning Strategy: Financial literacy begins with education and planning. Understanding income needs and potential pitfalls could help your clients avert many hardships later in life.

Yahoo! Sports, "From McDonald's All-American to McDonald's worker: How David Harrison lost his way after the NBA," March 13, 2015.

Lessons from the Boll Weevil
October 23, 2014

You may or may not be familiar with the story of the boll weevil, but I've been thinking about it the last few weeks during the recent market volatility. The story is a great reminder of why we need to consider alternative products outside of our normal assets-under-management mindset. Change is always feared, but many times, it results in greater success.

The boll weevil is a beetle that migrated to the United States from Mexico in the late 19th century and devastated the cotton crops in the

South. Farmers nearly went bankrupt due to the infestation, so many began to grow peanuts instead. Most cotton farmers resisted the change, however, saying peanuts wouldn't grow and no one would buy them. As it turns out, peanuts were not only resistant to the boll weevil, but they were also extremely profitable. In fact, the peanut farmers made enough money in three months to equal an entire year's work in cotton.

Eventually, the boll weevil was nearly eradicated in the south and cotton farming resumed. However, those who seized the opportunity to grow peanuts became far more prosperous than those who never diversified. In fact, the citizens of Enterprise, Alabama, erected a boll weevil monument to show their appreciation for the insect and its profound influence on the area's agriculture and economy.

Take a hint from the peanut farmers. With the recent market volatility, we must look to alternatives to meet client needs. Our clients continue to fear running out of money during retirement, yet we continue to throw out the same solutions to old problems. Like many farmers in the south found, a forced change creates opportunity and profits. Annuities and life insurance provide an opportunity to leverage tools for safety, protection and tax-advantaged growth. Many advisors don't like having a conversation about these products, but it's time to change.

Winning Strategy: The boll weevil taught a southern town the value of change. Adversity forces us to look at alternatives that many times work in our favor.

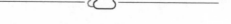

A Fresh Perspective
April 21, 2014

Recently, I spent the weekend in Houston, Texas. Most people would not think anything of it. However, after spending the last 16-20 weeks in northern Indiana with sub-freezing temperatures, the warmth of 80-degree days and sunshine made it feel like I was in a different world. I felt recharged, re-energized and refreshed with just a small change.

It made me think about our industry. How often do we as financial advisors get in a rut and need a fresh perspective? It seems we get in the habit of making successful sales presentations based upon one product filling a general solution. Too often, I hear advisors telling my firm they do not talk about longevity planning and insurance. Can we be so selfish and concerned about our own business as to not think it is our clients' business that we must focus on for success?

Yes, I speak and write about efficiency and effectiveness in financial services offices. But, it's time to make sure our clients' retirements and legacies remain effective and efficient, first and foremost.

For example, all of us have a responsibility to have a meaningful discussion with our clients about the impact of Congress' potential decision to accelerate the taxation on retirement accounts to the next generation. This might be the most destructive piece of legislation introduced, and I would guess that 90 percent of our clients are unaware of what Congress wants to do.

Clients expect leadership from their advisors. We must continue to earn their trust by having the difficult conversation that we don't want to have with them – the one about death and taxes. Positioning a client's assets for flexibility, income and estate planning should be our focus. That means that we need a fresh perspective with every client we meet, just like the change in temperature.

Winning Strategy: We must be up to date on our tax legislation, product offerings and solutions available for unique strategies. Focusing on those aspects important to the client will ultimately define our success as an industry.

Annuities and Sports:
What I learned from Coach Knight
November 13, 2014

I had the great honor of sitting at the end of the bench as a student manager for Indiana University's 1987 NCAA Championship men's basketball team. There are so many great memories associated with the basketball program and my time at IU. As schools kick off their basketball season over the next few weeks with midnight madness events, I typically use the basketball season to reflect on things that I learned from Coach Bob Knight that have made me successful in sales.

Measured Results – Success happens when you understand what works most often and under which circumstances. At IU, we kept multiple pages of statistics during routine, mundane practices. We filmed each practice for coaches to review the plays. The coaching staff knew which plays, sets and players performed well against a 2-3 zone, 3-2 zone or man-to-man defense. When it came time to make adjustments during a game, the coaches made intelligent moves instead of guesses. We were "consciously competent" as a program.

In sales, we have to make sure that we understand which clients have the greatest need for our products. More importantly, we have to understand their goals and how best to address the obstacles on their way to their goals.

Willingness to Prepare – One of my favorite and lasting quotes from Coach Knight is, "Everyone has a will to win; few have a will to prepare to win." During our tournament run, our team didn't leave the locker room thinking we wouldn't be coming back as a winner that day. We played Duke, LSU, UNLV, and Syracuse during the tournament. We had the same confidence throughout the season. Players and coaches worked diligently and spent extra time. We felt we had outworked every other team, and we felt we deserved to win.

In preparing to meet with a client or prospect, we need to have the same level of confidence that we can help our clients optimize their retirement and protection plans.

Play to Your Strengths – We all have strengths and weaknesses. Understanding and emphasizing our strengths maximizes our opportunity for success. Coaches taught the recognition of each of the players' strengths. For example, passing the ball to a 7-foot center near the free throw line was a mistake. Our center would have to take several dribbles to get into his shooting range, and dribbling was not his strength due to his size. That put the center in position to fail.

For me, I am not an emotional salesperson. It's not that I don't believe in our product – I have a deep commitment to the insurance industry and what it can do for clients. Instead, I've looked for clients who purchase on fact, not emotion. I've generated the most sales from those prospects making fact-based decisions. I've had to play to my strengths.

Collaborate with Professionals – I remember giving Coach Knight messages that mentors of his were returning his calls. People like Hank Iba (Oklahoma State and U.S. Olympic coach), Pete Newell (California and U.S. Olympic coach), and Everett Dean (Indiana and Stanford coach) were asked to provide input on players, the team and strategy.

As an industry, we need to collaborate more with other professionals. When I was in the field, working jointly with people in other specialties allowed me to deliver an entire team approach to my clients. The approach gave my clients the service and expertise they needed to feel confident they would have the financial success of their dreams.

Win with Integrity – During the four decades Coach Knight was head coach, his teams never had a major violation. When a player might have been involved with illegal recruiting at another program, more often than not Coach eliminated that player from consideration at IU.

Winning can be done within the rules. Understanding the rules and how to be successful within the guidelines allows success to happen. Our industry is full of regulations and rules – increasing every year. We have to find ways to make it easier to conduct business within these new rules and make our clients confident that they are making the right decisions.

Being part of a winning program led by a Hall of Fame coach provided me the foundation for business success. If our industry used some of the success principles of high-quality sports programs, I think we would perform differently. We would have the innovation like Google and Apple. We would have a focus on getting more people insured instead of protecting our distribution. Financial advisors would prepare their clients for catastrophes of life through the sale of insurance products.

Winning Strategy: In order to change, we must adopt the attitude of preparation – understanding where we have success, playing to our strengths and seeking open collaboration. Let's make this basketball season a season of change for our business.

Awareness Leads to Growth
June 5, 2014

Annuity Awareness should be an ongoing initiative for our industry – not just a focus in June. I read article after article about the complexities of annuities; however, when we explain to clients that annuities provide guarantees, protection from outliving their income and tax advantages, they easily understand. Advisors who engage their clients in annuity discussions get ahead of the game for several reasons.

- *An American turns 60 every 7.5 seconds.*[1] Think about that statistic for a moment ... and, think about the nearly unlimited pool of prospects who are looking for retirement income.

- *As of 2013, the ratio of Social Security covered workers to beneficiaries was reduced to 2.8.*[2] That means a lot less people are paying into Social Security, which places an undue amount of pressure on our entitlement programs. The need for self-reliance in America has never been greater, and at the same time, our average retirement account balances have never been lower.

- *Due to a variety of cultural, lifestyle and medical improvements, Baby Boomers will live 20-30 years after retirement.* That is in stark contrast to their parents, who typically lived for only 10-15 years. Given longer life expectancies, discussions about inflation have never been more important. Today's retirement conversations gain momentum with talk of stable income and growth on a depreciating asset.

In our industry, we spend a lot of time talking about the interest rate environment, regulation, compliance and product training. Regardless of the challenges and perceived impediments, the future holds unlimited possibilities. Americans need our services and products at unprecedented levels. It's up to us to help them.

Winning Strategy: Make yourself aware of all the opportunities. Once you consider them, you can't help but want to talk about using annuities to positively change a person's retirement.

[1]*Government Accountability Office, "Older Workers: Demographic Trends Post Challenges for Employers and Workers," 2001.*
[2] *Social Security Administration, "Ratio of Social Security Covered Workers to Beneficiaries, Calendar Years 1940-2013": https://www.ssa.gov/history/ratios.html*

Bankrupt Millionaires
May 19, 2014

Everyone dreams of living a lifestyle with millions of dollars of income, having people standing ready for your every move, and performing in front of thousands of people live – not to mention in front of millions via television. What's important, however, is how those millions of dollars are leveraged and positioned for the future. The worst seems to happen to the people with most.

Recently, many young men became instant millionaires due to their athletic abilities on the football field. Highly drafted NFL players can receive millions in bonuses and guaranteed salaries. Clearly, this seems like a lot for playing a game.

Unfortunately, these young men do very little to protect themselves and their investments. A staggering number of NFL players file for bankruptcy after retirement. And, the numbers are equally high for other professional athletes.

Professional athletes represent a microcosm of the American public. But still, a lack of understanding about finances creates the opportunity for poor decisions while we are employed. A discussion on the future and the need to protect what you have continues to be absent in most financial planning conversations. And finally, we fail to protect our clients against their own irrational behavior.

Winning Strategy: It's time to rethink how we educate individuals, advisors, and the general public. We have to prevent even our wealthiest clients from failure with protection from the unthinkable, guaranteed income for the future, and advice for how to use the blessings of today.

Beating Resistance

March 20, 2014

In early March, I attended the Society of Financial Service Professionals Leadership Development Conference. If you are a credentialed professional and have not looked at this organization, please do so. It is our industry's best-kept secret for professional growth and ethical accountability among peers. I enjoy spending time with advisors who have a common goal of seeking knowledge, building relationships and maintaining client interests above their own.

At the conference, I was reminded that most seasoned advisors experience resistance with clients and collaborative partnerships due to the complexity of client solutions. I was re-introduced to Gleicher's Formula for overcoming resistance:

$$D \times V \times F > R$$
- D = Dissatisfaction about the current situation
- V = Vision of how things could be in the future
- F = First steps necessary to change the outcome
- R = Resistance

This formula explains how to persuade anyone — including ourselves — to change behavior. Getting people to act is one of the most difficult things to accomplish in any sales or leadership role. However, by understanding the depth of a person's problem, we create urgency. The vision of how the problem can go away increases the likelihood for change exponentially. Even if the person doesn't perceive a problem exists, a clear vision of success may motivate change.

But, if clear first steps are not demonstrated, the formula does not produce enough value to overcome the resistance to change. Think of the first steps as a zero in the equation. Anything times anything times zero equals zero.

Winning Strategy: If you are looking to beat resistance, either external or internal, evaluate the severity of letting the current behavior continue against how much better the situation improves by the change. But most importantly, focus on the first step. It energizes change. Resistance will always be greater without action.

Build Momentum, Change the Game
September 12, 2014

As I was driving home from a recent trip, I listened to an NFL broadcast. It was so good to pass the time with a football game instead of music for once. Anyway, what struck me during the 3 ½ -hour drive was how many times the momentum changed during the game. You could hear it in the home team's announcers and sense it as one positive play built upon another.

In sales, much like football, momentum can change at a moment's notice. In football, momentum usually comes from a big play – a turnover, a big run, or a successful long pass. The players' confidence builds, and more big plays tend to follow.

In sales, why not control our momentum with big plays? When we're working on a lot of cases or have ones that we can dig our teeth into, we seem to have more momentum to call clients, bring up possible solutions or convey confidence in our proposals. How do we hold on to that momentum? With focus.

I encourage you to focus on one big play – one idea or strategy. Give it laser focus for the rest of the year. Laser focus means that you own the idea and can tell the story backwards and sideways, you have a defined target market to share the idea with, and you have the support to execute the idea with ease and confidence. When you're laser focused, you should definitely see a shift in momentum.

We have to change the momentum in our business. Life insurance ownership remains at industry lows, we continue to look the other way when it comes to protecting wealth from potential market corrections, and we fail to address the majority of Americans who continue to self-insure their long-term care contingent liability. Focus on one idea – one game-changing play – that can propel you for the rest of this year and springboard you into the next.

Winning Strategy: It just takes one idea or one sale to change the momentum in your business. Find the big play closest to your heart and run hard with it! Be a game-changer for the industry.

Concentration Kills Creativity
April 3, 2014

I am constantly surprised when I meet advisors around the country and discuss their concentration into one product or one carrier. Realizing that our presentations get better with repetition, we tend to stick with our comfort level and what worked most recently. Those factors lead to a routine, which leads to a high concentration in products or services. This concentration kills the creativity used in client solutions, which ultimately hurts our industry's end users.

If you were to audit your product preferences and carriers, would you find too much concentration in one offering? We spend a considerable amount of time examining our clients' portfolios for concentration risk. Are you doing the same thing for your business?

In the current interest rate environment, carriers have been forced to make changes to benefits, payout structures and income rider values. Today, there are more solutions available to meet the increasing demands of longevity protection. We have a responsibility to search for customized solutions for unique consumer goals and objectives.

It's time that we lose the comfort level for a specific product or carrier. Instead, we need to get comfortable with research, seeking knowledge and pursuing what best meets our clients' objectives.

Winning Strategy: I challenge all advisors to rethink their value to their clients. Our value should not be dependent on a product; our value needs to be our intellectual value of searching for the right solutions. Our concentration with one story might erode our value and creativity.

Don't Blame the Product – Work Harder!

March 13, 2014

"Don't wish it were easier; wish you were better."
– Jim Rohn

Prior to the 2014 Winter Olympics, the United States was favored to win several speed skating medals in Sochi. Shani Davis had won two gold medals at previous Olympic Games and was expected to win again. The United States medaled in every Games for the past 30 years, since the Sarajevo Games. Success seemed certain to some degree.

To provide an even more prolific advantage over the competition, the U.S. team began wearing "state-of-the-art" speed skating suits. And, to everyone's surprise, the Americans lost every skating event during the first week and won zero medals. An exception was granted to switch back to their old uniforms, but the results did not change. For the first time in 30 years, the U.S. speed skating team was shut out of any medals during an Olympic Games. A spotlight was placed on the uniform. It seems like the team members were hoping for the suits to make things easier; instead they were wishing they were more prepared.

Isn't it the same in sales? We all wish things would be different when we struggle. Sales is one of the most difficult professions due to the rejection, need for continual knowledge and focus on ever-changing prospects.

We spend a considerable amount of time, money and energy searching for the silver bullet. However, we need to concentrate on getting better.

Winning Strategy: Just like a change in uniform didn't make the U.S. speed skating team better, a new product or lead system doesn't make your job easier. It takes hard work, new ideas and commitment to the industry.

Experience Matters

April 7, 2014

The NCAA Final Four is an exciting place to be. It is often referred to as "The Pinnacle of College Basketball," and this year, Florida, Connecticut, Wisconsin and Kentucky climbed to the top. It takes talent, skill and – in some cases – a little luck to make it to the Final Four. The other component that shows up during post-season tournaments is experience.

Clearly, teams with pure talent can make it to the finals. For example, Kentucky has nine freshmen on its squad. But to really build a program, you need experience. Florida and Connecticut have senior point guards who are true leaders for their teams. Florida reached the Elite Eight the previous three years before reaching the Final Four this year, which is an unbelievable achievement. Connecticut has won previous national championships with quality senior guard play. And, Wisconsin has two seniors and a host of experienced juniors on its team.

The same is true for our industry. In order to build a financial services business that stands the test of time, you need experience behind you. Your firm may specialize in investments, wealth management or other facets of financial planning. To round out your offerings, you want experience to help drive the other arms of your clients' plans.

Winning Strategy: An experienced partner can help boost your firm's risk mitigation and overall insurance offerings.

Holding Money in the Right Pocket

July 7, 2014

Whether you like it not, your clients have likely made a very important financial decision without your input. Look at their investment portfolios – the absence of long-term care insurance indicates they elected to self-insure. They may not even know they made a decision, but they have. As advisors, we may not be able to change their decision, but we can help mitigate their risk.

Long-term care events may be the most costly risk to long-term accumulation and retirement goals. However, the majority of Americans have decided to avoid the purchase of stand-alone protection. Likely, it's too late for aging clients to consider this level of protection due to health concerns or an unwillingness to commit to high premiums.

If you're like me, you carry larger-than-normal amounts of cash when on vacation. You might place some money in your significant other's purse, in a suitcase or in multiple pockets. It's as if we're diversifying our vacation money, right?

Well, why don't we diversify our clients' risk by placing some of their "emergency bucket" money in the right pocket? Using asset-based tools, we can create leverage for our clients. While the return on these types of assets is low, the advantage is to remain in a conservative position while providing additional protection.

Winning Strategy: The next time you're looking at a portfolio and see no asset-based long-term care protection, ask your client if they have their money in the right pocket. I'm guessing that some of their portfolio is designated for future, costly medical events. Make sure you match up their assets with their risk and place the money where it can create the most leverage.

How Quickly It Goes ...

November 6, 2014

During the recent market volatility, it's hard to comprehend how much wealth was unnecessarily lost or how quickly. Through our complacency as advisors, our clients lost an astonishing amount of wealth that currently makes 2014 a nearly lost year. Due to inaction, we chose (yes, it was a choice not to have the conversations with our clients) to take them back to January 2014, when the S&P 500 was in a similar position.

Without a doubt, risks exist with equity investments. Up until the third quarter, investors were rewarded with better-than-average returns. However, we spoke earlier this year about the potential for a correction, or at least volatility. Once again, we failed to take gains off the table and protect our wealth.

Making clients aware of their options is paramount during bull markets. They never know how much risk to take ... until they've taken too much. We run the risk of repeating the mistakes and greed associated with the financial crisis of 2008-09.

In the 22 trading days since Sept. 18 – when the S&P 500 saw an all-time high of 2,011.36 – $787.3 billion of wealth has been lost. The U.S. Treasury's interest expense for debt payments was only $415 billion for all of 2013. In other words, we failed to protect more than 1.8 times the interest payment of the U.S. government.

Our clients should be appalled and question what they could have done differently. This time, let's have meaningful conversations about mechanisms that protect clients and minimize risk. An optimized retirement income isn't always dependent on the highest return or best asset allocation. An optimized retirement maximizes after-tax income, makes sure there are guarantees in place and places emphasis on protecting what we earn. Let's have the right conversations in the next bull market.

Winning Strategy: In the last month, clients lost more than a year's worth of national interest debt payments. In the future, we need to place more emphasis on protecting wealth.

Impact of Product Allocation

February 17, 2014

Financial services professionals always discuss the impact of asset allocation, but we rarely mention product allocation. How we use products can greatly enhance a client's solution and reduce risk – much like asset allocation. Using annuities in a portfolio can help reduce the pressure of withdrawals from a securities-based account.

Let's look at a typical retiree in the United States: Tony and Katherine have $750,000 in a managed account. Between the two of them, the couple anticipates $20,000 in Social Security income payments. The remaining $30,000 will be taken as systematic withdrawals from the managed account. The withdrawal represents a 4 percent distribution from the account. Over the years, the 4 percent distribution is likely to put a lot of pressure on the account if there is a repeat of 2008 or longer-than-expected life expectancies.

By adding additional products to the portfolio, Tony and Katherine can reduce the pressure on the managed account withdrawals. If they purchase a $150,000 joint-life immediate annuity with cash refund, the annuity generates nearly $9,000 in annual income. Using another $100,000 to buy an annuity with an income rider, the couple receives another $5,000 per year. The remaining $16,000 continues to be withdrawn from the managed account – now only a 3.2 percent distribution factor. The reduced distribution factor helps the couple in extended down markets, allows the managed account to grow more, and they still retain control of their assets and protect the beneficiaries.

Winning Strategy: Allocating a client's portfolio across different products, not just asset classes, can add significant value to the portfolio while providing guaranteed income for life – one of our clients' biggest fears. Look at alternatives before settling for the typical 4 percent distribution from managed accounts.

Innovation and Insurance
October 30, 2014

On Oct. 21, 1879, Thomas Edison invented the first commercially viable light bulb. It lasted 13.5 hours … but soon, the average bulb lasted 150 hours, and within 10 years, commercial bulbs glowed for 1,200 hours. The speed of improvement on Edison's commercial bulb was incredible.

Today, technology and communication are the new light bulb. Google, Apple and Microsoft have changed the way we live, communicate and do business. However, the insurance industry isn't catapulting like other industries with its speed of innovation. Why? Is it because we're full of mature carriers and distribution? It doesn't have to be that way, does it?

We have to look at new opportunities to expand and, at the same time, go back to our roots. Only 44 percent of Americans own life insurance outside of group contracts.* Why are we not addressing our own clients? What level of service are we providing to our existing clients?

Richard Branson started Virgin Airlines based on a bad service experience. The airline industry hasn't been the same since then. Which one of your clients will impact your business by leaving you, challenging you or becoming your competitor?

I challenge all distributors in our industry to force innovation. We can't continue to help Americans at the level they need without significant change. It requires investment, commitment and vision. Bringing new people into the business is only part of the solution; we have to change the way those new people interact with their clients. Within 10 years, we have to distribute products in a new way that can reach more people and grow, just like Edison's commercial light bulb.

Winning Strategy: Innovators like Thomas Edison and Richard Branson changed the way we live. Our industry must also change so Americans can continue to thrive after catastrophic events. The light bulb changed tenfold in 10 years; we have to do the same.

*LIMRA, "Facts About Life Insurance 2013," September 2013.

Lessons Learned on Mt. Everest

April 28, 2014

Recently, Mount Everest claimed 12 lives while Sherpas guided people toward the summit. It marked the deadliest day in the mountain's history, and 2014 is one of its deadliest years even though the climbing season has just started. Historically, most people lose their lives on Everest during their descent – not in their climb.

There are several risks associated with the descent. Fatigue is one of the biggest issues following the long climb to the summit. Falling behind the guides during the initial descent can lead to poor decisions or quick movements at high elevations. Descending too quickly creates a condition where fluid builds in the lungs. Ironically, most deaths have occurred during descents within 8,000 feet of the summit.

Financial professionals can use the descent of Everest as analogy for working with clients. They need to pay careful attention to several aspects of the process – they need to be attentive guides. First, the initial parts of the de-accumulation of assets are most critical. Mistakes in the early years of changing to the income phase can produce serious ripples throughout retirement. The sequence of returns plays a major role during these initial retirement years.

Second, clients tend to make quick decisions … usually because they haven't planned in the five to 10 years leading up to retirement. We must work with clients to reposition their assets to preserve and protect them in the descent from working years to retirement. One of the largest fears for most Americans is the transition from accumulating assets to depleting them.

Finally, we have to pay attention to our clients throughout retirement. The landscape fluctuates with rapid changes in market performance. We must keep our clients' best interests in mind and recognize that they prefer a steady income.

Winning Strategy: Annuities provide an income stream that creates steady, consistent income. They allow for the consistent disbursement of assets over a client's lifetime while averting one of their biggest fears – outliving their income. Taking away the risks of income early in retirement allows a planner to focus on longer-term asset growth to sustain inflation-protected income.

Looking for the Pothole Around the Corner

September 16, 2014

After the harsh winter of 2014, many streets were left with large and encompassing potholes. In my hometown, the city had to repave a stretch of a major downtown street because it was essentially impassable. With the Farmer's Almanac predicting an even a worse winter for 2015, we're already talking about the storms and havoc heading our way.

Unfortunately, we, as financial advisors, don't heed the same warnings, and we're positioned to repeat the same mistakes of the past. Today, many signs point to a market correction – a potential healthy correction of 10 percent or less. While it appears to be smaller than the financial crisis of 2008-09, it will nonetheless take trillions of dollars from investors.

Given that our clients are five to six years closer to retirement from last major correction, it should be more imperative to protect their wealth. Unfortunately, I continue to hear advisors satisfied with their clients' account values and assets under management going up without regard to risk and the opportunity to mitigate those risks.

With today's product portfolios, many advisors miss the opportunity to lock in gains from existing accounts, especially retirement accounts. I would estimate that 50 percent of our clients would like to take the gains from the last five years off the table and make sure they don't repeat the claw back they experienced in 2008-09.

While fixed annuity returns remain low, the risk associated with a potential market correction would outweigh the loss in account value. Look at your client base. Which ones called you the most or came to you as a new client during the last correction? Talk to them about their interest in taking some of their gains off the table. You'll be looking out for their potential pothole around the corner.

Winning Strategy: Many clients have recovered from the financial crisis of five years ago, and they'd like to protect what they've gained. Contact them now to help take those gains off the table.

Performance and Price are Irrelevant

October 7, 2014

Too often, we become focused on the price or performance of a particular solution we offer. Whether it's annual premium or return to the client, we allow it to dictate the conversation with price-sensitive parameters. Currently, there is a great example of how price, performance and return to the client really don't matter in the industry. Instead, it's about vision, leadership and perspective.

The PIMCO Total Return Bond Fund has been an industry Goliath for years.

	1 Year	3 Year	5 Year	10 Year
PIMCO Total Return (Class A)	5.71%	3.88%	5.21%	5.65%
Barclay's U.S. Aggregate	5.66%	2.91%	4.48%	4.72%

Yet, $23.5 billion left the bond fund giant in September. The previous industry record outflows were $9.7 billion and $4.7 billion. So, a fund with superior performance lost $23.5 billion dollars (the majority of that happened last Friday after Bill Gross's resignation) in one month.

What does this tell us? Investors and clients really don't care about price and performance. They're seeking leadership.

Be a strong voice in your business. Position yourself as the go-to person in your market and provide leadership to your clients. Lead them down a path of discovery to understand insurance and annuities are vital to their retirement plan.

Winning Strategy: As the PIMCO example illustrates, it's not about performance – it's about belief and perception. We have to change the perception of life insurance and annuities in financial plans. We have to tell the story and get the client to believe in our leadership and ideas.

———————— ⌒○ ————————

Planning with May in Mind
May 12, 2014

In my hometown of Indianapolis, Indiana, the month of May brings spring, warmer temperatures and the Indianapolis 500. The Indy 500 is celebrating its centennial era after the inaugural race of 1911. Much has changed, but many of its traditions remain intact. Because of the race, May contains a lot of tradition, pageantry and speed. And, if we are lucky, sometimes late May has some NBA Playoff action.

The events of May are a great analogy for talking to your clients about their retirement plans and future income needs. Teams are looking for speed, endurance and strategy throughout the month.

At the beginning of the month, the focus is on speed in order to qualify for the best starting position. Many of our clients retire with plans to travel, build new vacation homes or start new businesses. These early retirement years require a lot of income, and sometimes, we need to look at the most tax efficient manner to fund these years. Positioning our clients for their best start requires planning and strategy for the 10-15 years prior to retirement.

In the Indy 500, teams who don't test regularly struggle with qualifying and end up starting at the back of the 33 cars. The turbulence at the back of the pack is incredible, so getting your clients near the front is critical. Provide them with options for retirement by having a different conversation about protection, guaranteed income levels and diversifying the product portfolio.

After qualifying for Indy, teams begin looking for endurance. Drivers and machines must last a grueling 500 miles at speeds averaging 210-plus mph. Each team is provided the same amount of fuel and tires, and they must meet the same technical specifications. How they utilize the allowable resources throughout the race determines how they finish. We have to make sure our clients use their available resources appropriately and have a plan that will last for their entire life with certainty.

Finally, in the final 50 laps or so of the race, strategy plays a large role in determining who reaches the winner's circle. Making sure our clients have multiple streams of income that they can't outlive is only one part of winning their retirement race. One of the most overlooked needs in retirement planning is inflation protection. Today, interest rates are poised to increase at some point the next three to five years. Therefore, the ability to afford the same items and maintain a normal lifestyle in the future requires growing your income. It's easier to grow income with the proper products than to grow your account balances above and beyond your withdrawal rate annually and consistently.

Winning Strategy: In order to win the retirement race, it takes planning, education, communication with your clients, and strong product selection.

Resetting Expectations
June 9, 2014

Today's advisors continue to be bombarded with negative headlines about fixed income solutions. The media harps on the low-interest-rate environment to the point that advisors and clients fear making a mistake on timing, resulting in lost opportunity.

The reality is, standing on the sidelines is the true lost opportunity.

What needs to happen for the industry to grasp that we are closer to normal, long-term interest rates than we are to low ones? The historical average during the entire 20th century was 4.9 percent. Looking at the past 50 years, the average on the first 25 years was 3.3 percent, and it rifled upward during the late '70s and early '80s. The average for the second half of the period was only 6.7 percent – double the average in a period that included 15 percent interest and inflation rates.

Today, long bonds have yields around 3.5 percent. Clearly, we are closer to normal than many would like us to believe.

It's time to reset expectations. Today's interest rates remain in line with the amount of risk taken. For clients who want zero risk, fixed annuities and fixed indexed annuities are a great alternative. And, in the unlikely event of skyrocketing rates in the next year, annuities provide a shelter for price depreciation.

Winning Strategy: Let's have meaningful conversations with our clients about the virtue of annuities in our "new normal."

Safety and Control
July 10, 2014

In a well-documented study decades ago, British scientists set out to determine how a worker's position on the corporate ladder corresponded to their stress level. It was assumed that more responsibility led to more stress, which in turn led to more incidents of serious health care issues.

The Whitehall Studies produced some interesting findings. Workers higher on the corporate ladder were actually less stressed, due to the amount of control they had during the day. And a worker's responsibility had nothing to do with stress-related health issues.

I would argue that the same can be said about retirement planning. The amount of money involved is irrelevant. When an individual feels uncomfortable about their income stream, that uncomfortable feeling translates into stress, which increases the probability of problems.

Imagine your stress if you become a burden to your family members. Unfortunately, that stress will begin to form many years before you run out of money or have health issues. Without guaranteed income, you risk being a burden. Because of risks like this, a retiree's stress level can become unbearable.

Annuities can prevent most of this stress. While the return is not in the range of equities, the power of safety promotes comfort and control. And, when individuals feel in control of their future, they feel less stressed.

Winning Strategy: Just as control at work could ease a worker's stress, I believe Americans would benefit from the safety and comfort of a conversation with their financial advisor.

Shopping vs. Saving

March 27, 2014

While reading some research data, I read an amazing, nearly unbelievable, quote from a KRC Research project sponsored by TIAA-CREF. It read, "Americans prefer choosing a restaurant or buying a TV over IRA planning."* What's more disturbing is that 55 percent of respondents take an hour or less per year planning for retirement.

We have roughly 201,480 hours (or an average of 23 years) of retirement. So, with less than an hour each year during our working years, we spend less than 44 hours planning for 201,480 hours of our lives. That is two ten-thousandths of the time. Add health care, inflation and taxes to the mix, and that time invested seems unreasonably short.

How can we feel comfortable in our retirement years without the proper planning? The trends grow worse, according to the survey. Only 17 percent of Americans are contributing to IRAs now, compared to 22 percent two years ago. Of the people not contributing to IRAs, only 47 percent of respondents would consider making contributions now.

As an industry, we can't blame our clients. We have a done a poor job of motivating people to save. We have become complacent with our assets under management and lost focus on our true responsibility — making sure our clients have confidence and can maintain a successful retirement. There are too many risks to be discussed: long-term care funding, longevity planning and inflation protection. These three topics require at least one to two hours of discussion.

Winning Strategy: It's time we refocus on the client, educating Americans on the risks in front of them, and providing solutions they may not be aware are available to them. Let's get back to the basics and talk about how our industry can eliminate risk to maximize our clients' chances for success.

* *TIAA-CREF IRA Survey, March 13, 2014.*

The Domino Effect

February 24, 2014

Traveling in the Midwest these past few weeks has been less than easy. I almost thought John Candy and Steve Martin were following me through my planes, trains and automobiles.

At the gate, I almost decided to leave the airport, thinking my first flight would not catch the connecting flight. However, as I stepped away from the gate, the flight began boarding and I made a last-minute decision to get on the plane. As feared, I missed my connecting flight to Buffalo, New York; instead, the airline shipped me to my next day's appointment in Milwaukee and, after my flight from Milwaukee was canceled, I ended up driving five hours to get home.

It seemed as though the first flight set off a chain of events that resonated throughout the rest of my trip. In retirement planning, we call this sequencing of returns.

Having several bad investment performance years over a 30-year retirement cycle is usually not a deal-breaker. However, if those negative years occur at the beginning of retirement, the consequences can linger. So, many times, advisors use an analysis with an average return. If you take the average and place the best years first and/or the worst years first, the account value hits zero in a range of 13 years' difference. So, it's important to take the risk of a poor sequence of returns out of your clients' equation, especially early in the retirement years.

If I had this week's travel to do over, I certainly would have continued walking away from the gate. Make sure your clients walk away from the gate of potential pitfalls and unknowns.

Winning Strategy: By placing part of your clients' portfolio in a guaranteed growth and guaranteed income stream, you help eliminate the initial sequence of returns. By eliminating that first potential downfall, you have positively impacted the chances of your client having a successful retirement.

The Value of Financial Advice

February 13, 2014

I read an article recently discussing how the term "wealth management" was being misused. The article focused on how clients perceived the term in relation to how much they were paying in fees. I have always objected to this type of thinking. How we describe ourselves as professionals should be defined through our core values, not by how we are compensated or our business model.

In the past decade, much has been written about the value of fee-based planners over commission-based agents and/or advisors. I network with many advisors using different compensation models; many use fee-based planning models while many use a commission-based model. Both groups not only provide quality service to their clients but they also meet their needs. There are many instances where insurance needs cannot be met with the limited fee-only products. And, there are many client goals that can be met with just fee-only, assets under management account.

It's time to re-think the value of advice and define it by the level of competence, expertise and integrity toward the client. Our industry must get to the point where lobbyists and regulators relinquish the power to define professionalism, and make it about how our clients perceive successful client/advisor relationships by exceeding expectations, regardless of how we are compensated.

Winning Strategy: Working with a financial professional needs to be a personal choice built on relationship, trust and a confidence that the professional will exceed the clients' expectation. All of those things can be completed with various compensation models.

What if You Do Not Act

July 14, 2014

Many articles and news reports have covered the Federal Reserve's concern about the apparent investor complacency bubble. Based on the market, I believe it to be a legitimate concern. We have higher-than-normal price-to-earnings ratios and all-time market highs, and the annuity industry is similar to that of the pre-financial crisis.

Given that the normal P/E ratio is around 16 for the S&P 500, we are approximately 20 percent overvalued in the stock market. When you look at the baby boomers, how many can sustain their standard of living if their retirement assets decreased by 20 percent in the next 90 days? My guess is many would suffer a nearly unrecoverable decrease in their standard of living.

More importantly, what is the psychological effect on those pre-retirees who have been battling to get back to their pre-financial crisis retirement accumulation? This generation has spent the last decade pushing a large boulder up the hill. Boomers have felt the impact of 9/11, the technology bubble, the financial crisis and now an apparent complacency bubble. Why would we let our clients continue to make the same mistakes?

It's time we stop waiting for interest rates to increase or for there to be a "better deal." Doing nothing only perpetuates the risk that is already being taken. If we don't protect our clients' assets and wealth, they're likely to repeat the same errors over and over again. Let's get off the merry-go-round and help them.

Winning Strategy: Ask for meetings with your top clients to talk about taking their risk off the table and protecting their wealth. If you don't, someone else might do it for you.

When Did We Lose Our Way?

September 30, 2014

I arrived home and picked up about three days' worth of mail. When I picked up Insurance News Net magazine, I was shocked to see the headline, "How to add AUM Now." And, AUM was emphasized in bright colors. While I know that this publication supports all facets of our industry, it is clearly supported by risk mitigation products.

Sadly, I think this is indicative of our industry. We have drifted so far toward AUM, which by the way stands for assets under management, that we have lost our way. I have some questions:

- When did we lose sight of what got us into the business?
- At what point did we sell our souls to accumulation and wealth building?
- How did wealth management translate into just growing assets and not truly managing wealth?

As an industry, we need to get back to talking about life insurance, disability income, long-term care and longevity insurance. We can no longer talk, promote and focus on growing assets alone. In today's economic environment, protecting assets should be more important than growing them.

We all have a responsibility to make advisors aware of the growing gap in Americans' ownership of protection products. It begins with each one of us looking in the mirror and asking if we have the clients' very best interests in mind when we focus on growing assets and not protecting lives. It begins with carriers focusing on new product development with ongoing commission to eliminate the exchanges of products and supporting annual reviews. It begins with a changing mindsets.

Winning Strategy: When did we sell out to asset management as a business model versus what got us into the business?

Have You Adopted the Forward Pass?

December 10, 2015

In football, the forward pass is a must by today's standards. In fact, the highest producing NFL offenses are built around the ability to throw the ball around the field. But it wasn't always that way. The game changed significantly in 1905 when the forward pass was approved for play ... but not every team adopted the new rules immediately.

In the early 1900s, football was pretty much a running game. Because of this, concussions and head injuries were very common. One year, 18 deaths occurred on the football field due to the severity of the game. To make football less violent and safer for college students, Teddy Roosevelt worked with school leaders to figure out new rules. Thus, the forward pass was instituted.

Unfortunately, not every school took to the forward pass quickly. Initially, if a player dropped a pass, it was a turnover, and if a pass was caught in the end zone, it was a touch-back. If a pass didn't go five yards, it resulted in a 15-yard penalty. Risks were high in being different.

Saint Louis University's Eddie Cochem instituted the forward pass into his offense in 1906, when most colleges continued to run the ball. They won their next game, 22-0. Pop Warner began to use the forward pass at a small college, Carlisle Indian Industrial School, in 1907. His teams outscored their competition 148-11 over the first five games of the season. Then, tiny Carlisle took on the University of Pennsylvania football team using the forward pass. Pop Warner's team beat the mighty school in front of 22,800 fans by a score of 26-6. While that score is decisive, the yardage gain was even more lopsided. Carlisle outgained Penn 402 to 76 yards that afternoon.

The new wave of offense was noticed by bigger eastern schools, and the forward pass began to gain traction.

What's my point in all this? We need to look toward the innovators within our industry. Using the same withdrawal strategies for our clients will no longer work in economic environments where bond prices and rates are unpredictable, life expectancies are increasing rapidly, and volatility creates anxiety. It's just like running the football into the middle of the line and getting crushed.

We have to look for new ways to make sure our clients are safe. No rule, legislation or single product can solve the concerns and multiple risks of so many Americans. Instead, financial professionals have to use combinations of products and tools to meet the income demands of retirees. If your client's retirement income isn't safe, it's time to change the game and look for new ways to play the game.

Winning Strategy: You can't win the game running the same old offense that won in the past. Times have changed, economics have changed, and client attitudes have changed. Innovate and look for new ways to help your clients win in retirement.

Observe. Seek Data. Share It.
December 17, 2015

Recently, I traveled to Philadelphia, Pennsylvania, where our firm hosted Thrive University with Curtis Cloke. It was a high-level training session for serious planners in the income planning marketplace. The attendees (myself included) gained a lot of valuable insights, several of which I realized are echoed by a book, "Misbehaving: The Making of Behavioral Economics," by Richard H. Thaler.

Nearly three decades ago, Thaler was a lone wolf talking about behavior economics and the effects of client behavior. Over the last 30 years, he's gleaned a few key takeaways:

- **The power of observation** – "The first step to overturning conventional wisdom is to look at the world around you"
- **The importance of collecting data** – "To really convince yourself, much less others, we need to change the way we do things: we need data, and lots of it"
- **The criticality of speaking your mind** – Thaler brought about change by being prepared to speak up himself, but he also stressed the need for all of us to speak up

What's the takeaway for us as financial professionals? A few things.

1. **Observe.** Look around you and your clients. We are – and likely will remain – in an overall low-interest-rate environment. Today's economy is drastically different than the late 1990s and early 2000s. We live in a more volatile market. The question in income planning is no longer, "How can we mitigate risk with asset allocation?" but instead, "How can we shift the risk through product allocation?" Client demographics continue to change around us and expectations have changed as well.

2. **Seek data.** We don't know what we don't know, so we always have to be willing to learn. Thrive University, for example, opened the eyes and minds of many of the attendees. One advisor said, "I need to go back and have a conversation with all my clients about this philosophy." Curtis helped us remember the importance of nominal versus real returns, implied yield comparisons, fee drag and tax impact – components that make a strong income plan for life.

3. **Share it.** In the early stages of behavior economics, Thaler went against the grain. While the topic is growing, it's important we help continue the message. The fact is, our clients do NOT act rationally. Because of irrational behavior, we must set bumpers in their financial plans to provide guidance and a level of safety in income. But, it's important for all of us to look the two points above, recognize that we need to change our mindset, and, as an industry, change the way we deliver inflation-adjusted income to our clients.

Winning Strategy: By admitting that our clients need a different strategy and taking time to work *on* our business, not *in* it, we will change the security level of many Americans in their retirement. Look around at the changes, seek answers with an open mind and change the level of security for many of your clients.

Why Financial Professionals Will Matter Post-DOL

December 24, 2015

Recently, while on a plane, I read a quick article on Money Observer, a British financial site.* It was like I was getting a glimpse into the future of the post-DOL world here in the United States. With similar regulations taking effect in the United Kingdom in 2012, many clients can't afford financial advice.

Two facts in the article were staggering:

1. Half of the respondents who had an idea of how they were going to take their retirement savings thought that a draw-down strategy (systematic withdrawal strategies) would provide guaranteed income for life. Unfortunately, there are many variables that affect that strategy, including rates of return and withdrawal rates. But, I can confidently say that it will not guarantee income for life.

2. Twenty-five percent of respondents thought the draw-down strategy was risk free. Clearly, there's a gap in the fundamental mechanics of receiving income from pensions. To a lesser extent, I found it interesting that 25 percent of respondents thought their pension income was tax-free.

The complexities of the British pension system are no different than the complexities of U.S. retirement plans. Regardless, it's clear that Americans will need advice.

With some of the DOL ruling leaking out in various presentations over the last 30 days, I think it's important not to lose sight of where commission-based products fit into the proposed rule (and, I stress that as of now it's still a proposed rule), which makes an attempt to focus on what is best for the client. We can't let paperwork and regulation get in the way of what many of us have been doing for years – putting the client first and making sure there is a baseline of guaranteed income.

Educating people and putting them in the right position to make quality decisions will never go out of favor. Because of that, I encourage financial professionals to think about how they will educate the large portion of retirement asset holders who will no longer have a wealth manager tied to the asset. Their clients will be looking for quality education, expertise and recommendations that will impact their lives for the next 30-plus years.

Let's collectively step up to the challenge of a post-DOL world and make a difference for our clients, their families, their co-workers and our industry. Don't let the fear of change and how we transact business affect our view of who we do business with our or how our advice should be disseminated.

Winning Strategy: While we may need to be more transparent and change forms, we shouldn't lose our core value proposition to our clients: quality advice and sensible solutions, delivered consistently through personal interaction.

Money Observer, "Would you trust a robot at retirement? Financial Futures," Nov. 10, 2015.

What 'Sesame Street' Can Teach Us About Selling
December 31, 2015

On Nov. 10, 1969, Joan Ganz Cooney debuted a new children's program on public television. Up to that point, she'd been a documentary filmmaker. However, her true love was education-based television, and she wanted to create something that would resemble the highly popular "Rowan and Martin's Laugh In." She hired a gentlemen named Jim Henson to create puppets – "Sesame Street" was born.

Many of us grew up with Jim Henson's characters, and they still resonate today. "Sesame Street" not only taught you about letters and numbers, but could also teach you a thing or two about selling. The show's success can be attributed to several of Joan's strategies:

- Segments were short and to the point – it layered education and leveraged repetition

- They used various media – animation, human actors and puppets
- Shows were generally upbeat and fun

When working with clients, think how you can use those elements to be successful:

In today's world of distractions, we have to be to the point. We're trying to build long-lasting relationships, but our clients think in short bursts of attention. Let things build with time and repetition.

Find ways to best communicate with each client or prospect. The options are endless – emails, letters, phone calls, brochures, handouts, slides, videos … the list goes on. You have to be prepared because clients are doing their research before they ever meet you.

We must remain positive. While we have a responsibility to discuss the "not so pleasant" realities of life, there's no reason to be negative about any products, services or circumstances. During periods of volatility and economic uncertainty, our clients want someone to look them in the eye and tell them, "It's going to be OK" or, "This is what we need to do right now." No website or robo-advisor can do that for them.

Winning Strategy: Simple usually wins. Think about making things "Sesame Street" simple for your clients to understand. It will improve your communication and your impact.

Shaping our Business for Success
January 14, 2016

In the annuity industry, 2016 continues to shape up as a year of change and challenge. With the proposed U.S. Department of Labor (DOL) ruling anticipated to be announced this spring, many are wondering how they should set their goals, transition their business to advisory platforms or build out separate units for Middle America. In reality, we need to focus on some of the basic tenants of goal planning.

You probably know you need to keep goals SMART – Specific, Measurable, Attainable, Realistic and Timely. In times of significant change, we must keep those guidelines in mind as we set a new course for many of our businesses in the annuity industry.

Specific – We need to have a vision of what our financial planning practices will do for clients. Even under a fiduciary standard, it's hard to imagine being all things to all clients. We must get specific about what services we want to provide to clients at an exceptional level.

Measurable – There are many metrics that will allow you to keep score and stay on track throughout the year. In times of change, we might have several parallel goals. Of course, we need to have a total sales or revenue goal. But, you might want to think about how much of your business you want to transition before the end of the year, or have another metric in mind.

Attainable – Because we are looking into a muddy crystal ball with a new regulator and unannounced rule, it is difficult to judge attainability. Clearly, we must set a course for a fiduciary standard sometime in 2017. I think it's important to keep in mind that the sooner we shift our planning to this standard, the more attainable our goals will be once the ruling is finalized this spring.

Realistic – Realistic goals begin with action – early and often. We can no longer sit and wait for a legislative bailout in the 11th hour. Setting realistic expectations with clients and staff begins immediately. Slowly, we'll start learning to have transparent conversations with clients; by year end, we'll transition into deeper conversations about how our industry earns revenue for our expert advice.

Timely – We must set our goals with an end date in mind. With so much in flux with regulatory change, you should consider setting your goals at 90-day increments. We should know the final ruling by spring 2016. This allows the industry to set goals for the transition to a fiduciary standard by Jan. 1, 2017.

Winning Strategy: Goals are important, but we just can't focus on sales this year. In order to create long-term success in our industry, we must focus on our written policies and procedures to create meaningful goals that will transform our practices. By working on transparency and planning in 2016, we'll provide ourselves with a jumpstart on our new post-DOL world.

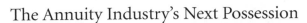

The Annuity Industry's Next Possession

January 28, 2016

While serving as a student manager for the men's basketball team at Indiana University, I learned a lot from Coach Bob Knight. Many of those lessons can be applied to the financial industry, and I've written about a few before. Today, as we're on the cusp of what could be a game-changer for our industry, I wanted to share another.

Missing the Long Shot

Once, during a practice, a star player took an open three-point shot and missed. Like most long shots, it resulted in a long rebound and a fast break for the opponents. That's embarrassing enough, but to make matters worse, the player (like many college athletes) stopped and hung his head. His delayed reaction gave his opponents an advantage on the fast break, resulting in a layup.

Coach Knight immediately stopped practice. "What just happened?" he asked. Well first of all, the shot was missed for a variety of reasons. But, that was in the past – there was nothing the play could have done to change the shot after it left his hands. He could have reacted to the rebound, however.

You see, after a missed shot, the shooter actually has an advantage – more than anyone else on the court, he has the best feel for where the rebound is heading. If he's paying attention, he can get in position to stop the ensuing fast break. Unfortunately, if he chooses to dwell on his missed shot, even for a second, it can result in an easy bucket for the other team. And we know one bucket can win or lose a game.

Getting Back on Defense

Today, our industry is in the same position as a player who misses a long shot. Over the last several years, we have successfully fought several pieces of legislation that would have affected the annuity industry. However, with the pending U.S. Department of Labor (DOL) ruling, it appears more likely than not that we will be required to maintain a fiduciary standard for every qualified client.

Sure, there will be litigation and other efforts to change the DOL's proposed ruling, but it's a long shot (pun intended). Regardless, it's clear we will need to change in the annuity industry.

That's OK. We can't hang our heads for a split second, allowing litigators to attack our individual businesses under the fiduciary rule. Instead, we have to get back on defense and get ready for the next possession.

Defense means changing how we DOCUMENT business, not how we DO business. I've heard many financial planners planning to discontinue the use of certain financial vehicles because of the commission structure. But if a product or service is in the best interest of a client, we should be obligated to implement the recommendation, regardless of our compensation structure.

Setting Up the Offense

We simply have to explain how the product works and how we get paid. Our clients want us to succeed as much as we do. They will understand the need for compensation if they understand how the product benefits them and their financial situation. Once we document and explain, we can move toward implementation – which means we're back on offense.

Winning Strategy: Don't hang your head and let regulation and changes to the industry affect how you do business. Get to the next possession so you can continue to help your clients.

What Circumstances Really Do For You
February 4, 2016

This past Christmas, I received the book, "Sidelined," as a gift from my mother-in-law, and I was inspired when I read it. The book is about Chuck Pagano, who battled cancer during his first season as head coach of the Indianapolis Colts. It's a story of family, faith and vision that rings true for everyone, including financial professionals.

Coach Pagano was named head coach of the Colts in January 2012.

Not long into his first season, he was diagnosed with leukemia and started cancer treatment, forcing him to take a leave of absence from his coaching duties. Pagano's family – both his blood relatives and his football family – helped keep his spirits high.

Throughout his treatment, he kept telling himself one thing:

> *"But regardless of our circumstances, they do not define us –*
> *not unless we give in and let them. Circumstances never*
> *determine who we are; they reveal who we are."*
> *– Chuck Pagano*

Today, Coach Pagano remains cancer-free and in full remission.

Reveal Yourself

Ask yourself, "How are my circumstances defining me and/or my financial services practice?" Maybe a broker-dealer is defining how you serve your clients. Maybe your perception of certain products and services within our industry are affecting your financial plans. Or, maybe the circumstances of pending regulation and the uncertainty around new standards are making you unsure of your entire practice.

There will always be changes in our industry – some more drastic than others. However, we can't let those circumstances define us. Instead, each change provides a chance for us to reveal our true value to the American public – providing quality advice to help generate dependable, secure income that our clients can't outlive.

Those professionals who hold their clients' best interests front and center will thrive in our new transparent world. No one should hesitate to earn a commission or charge a fee so long as the service and/or product meets the best interest of the client.

The commission structure of a financial solution is largely irrelevant. What that solution does and how it fits into the individual's financial plan is what matters most.

That, I believe, is what our circumstances will reveal about our industry.

Winning Strategy: Don't let your circumstances define you. Instead, let them REVEAL you.

Plan for Retirement's Descent
February 11, 2016

Climbing Mt. Everest is one of the most sought-after adventures in the world. Since Sir Edmund Hillary reached the top in 1953, more than 4,000 different climbers have reached the summit a total of 6,871 times. And, since 2000, the number of climbers has increased dramatically due to the commercialization of expeditions on the mountain.

Unfortunately, deaths on Mt. Everest have increased as well, and more than half of them occur on the descent from the summit, not the climb. Why? Most people focus on the time, energy, resources and support needed to reach the top. Few pay as much attention to what's needed to make it back down.

The same can be said about retirement planning. Americans spend a considerable amount of energy and resources to save for a successful retirement. However, most of us don't think about what we'll do once we get there. Sure, we need to have those assets. But, a large factor in our retirement success is how we use those assets once our income starts.

Facing the Risks

The early retirement years magnify several risks – longevity, sequence of returns and inflation, to name a few. Addressing these concerns during the climb to retirement can make your clients' descent much more smooth, reliable and efficient.

Longevity – This is the multiplier of all other retirement risks. Making sure clients have reliable income reduces the impact longevity can have a portfolio.

Sequence of Returns – We can't control what will happen to the market during the early years of retirement. But, we can take steps to insulate portfolios from this risk and provide greater probability that funds will last longer.

Inflation – We have to make sure our client's income base can grow as they age. They must be confident they can afford the same necessities today AND in 25 years.

Winning Strategy: Make sure you plan for the descent while you're helping clients climb to their retirement. Consider the risks and plan a retirement income strategy that helps them come down from the retirement summit safely.

What We Must do to Turn Crisis into Opportunity
February 18, 2016

The Chinese symbol for crisis is a popular metaphor that's been used by leaders and motivational speakers for years. The word is often said to be made of two distinct symbols – danger and opportunity – though that interpretation isn't entirely correct.

The first symbol, "wēi," does mean dangerous or precarious. However, the second symbol, "jī," translates more accurately to something like "critical point." That still seems fitting, in my opinion, as we find ourselves at a dangerous and critical point in the financial services industry.

With the pending fiduciary standards from the U.S. Department of Labor (DOL), we're at a junction where regulation meets client service. The critical point we must maneuver is implementing the required fiduciary standards and conflict of interest rules while building our businesses. Fortunately, I believe many of us are currently doing this and will be largely unaffected. However, the noise around this ruling creates angst of what the future holds.

Everyone should stay focused on the critical points in the discussion:

- **We must act in the best interest of our clients.** You're probably doing this already, but I find many advisors are closed-minded when it comes to looking at diverse product options. This bias will need to change. It will be critical to find quality partners who can open our minds to new solutions for our clients.

- **We must use fair and balanced language with clients.** Again, I believe most of the industry is meeting this requirement. However, we will have to up our game and have deeper discussions about how products meet the clients' needs, and we will need to examine the other options we considered with the client in mind. The result might be a slightly longer sales cycle, but a more informed client.

- **We must discuss compensation.** While this will be uncomfortable at first, we must learn to tell our clients how we are compensated for delivering valuable services to them. That means we will have to tie our compensation to the value we are providing – directly and indirectly.

Yes, we are at a dangerous and critical point in our business. However, this crisis can lead to opportunity if we keep the critical points clear and in focus. Let's make sure we address them, then move forward with helping our clients meet their financial goals.

Winning Strategy: Crisis means different things. But, with focus and clarity, we can turn crisis into opportunity. Make sure you focus on the changes you need to in order to have success.

Debunk Your Biases

February 25, 2016

Early in January, an article from Forbes presented some potential concerns about annuities. Titled, "4 Red Flags to Watch Out for Before Buying an Annuity," (Jan. 9, 2016) it seemed focused on products that have longer and higher surrender charges. Since these products represent a very small percentage of the market, I wanted to spend some time focusing on the basics of the products we use to help improve our clients' retirement success.

First of all, we must remember that annuities are long-term products designed for retirement income. Your clients can use a portion of their income to purchase a guaranteed stream of income – potentially for life – which is backed by the financial strength and claims-paying ability of the issuing insurance company. With the basics in mind, there are several client benefits:

Tax Deferral

Our products allow the accumulation value to grow while not being subject to tax during the accumulation period. The client is only taxed on the growth when they withdraw the gain from the contract. Of course, for this benefit, tax penalties apply on certain withdrawals prior to age 59 ½.

Guaranteed Income

One of the largest risks in retirement is longevity risk – living so long you run out of money. Some of our products carry an option to convert the accumulation value to a lifetime stream of income, regardless of the remaining account value. This transfer of risk can help ensure your clients won't run out of money. It's important to remember, however, that these long-term products should not be for the entire portfolio, just a portion.

Guaranteed Growth

Because traditional fixed annuities are contractual agreements between a client and an insurance company, many contracts carry a guaranteed minimum interest rate. Many times, these guarantees are higher than prevailing interest rates on taxable instruments. Check your local interest rates against highly rated insurance carriers' interest rates to make a decision on which contracts might be more attractive for your client. Due to the carrier providing these guarantees, most insurance contracts require the contract to be held a certain number of years. Make sure your client's objectives meet the holding period in order to not be charged a penalty from the insurance company.

Low Fees

As mentioned above, many tax-deferred vehicles require a holding period before the contract is 100 percent free of any withdrawal charges. That holding period allows the insurance carrier to invest 100 percent of the client's premium with no upfront sales charge. Over time, this initial savings can impact the overall growth of the contract for the client. With newer products that are linked to an external index, clients need to understand the limitations on growth potential each product has as the insurance company is guaranteeing the principal.

Clearly, our financial products have both advantages and

disadvantages. Each client scenario might call for different solutions; however, annuities may be a suitable fit for many clients, especially those concerned about running out of money in their lifetime. Don't rely on what you've heard about these products. Instead, give a fair and balanced assessment to whether they can help meet the client's objectives.

Winning Strategy: Don't allow media bias to affect how and when you might use an annuity with a client. There are solid reasons to look toward an annuity to solve many client situations.

The Key to Success is Simple
March 10, 2016

Simplicity seems to be hitting me in the face with a two-by-four. After attending a conference with a speaker focusing on simplicity, on my flight home I read some recaps of college basketball games I had missed. Again, simplicity was identified as the theme for success.

As many of you know, I follow the Indiana Hoosiers – especially their basketball program. This season started with high hopes, followed by a lot of doubt after the team lost two games in the Maui Invitational. Then, the Hoosiers were completely run out of the gym when they played the Duke Blue Devils at Cameron Indoor Arena. Before they even played a conference game, their season of hope turned into a season of frustration.

Even worse, our second-leading scorer was out for the season after a non-contact injury in practice around Christmas. So younger, less experienced players were inserted into the line-up. In order to give them a better chance for success, their offensive scheme was made simpler. The players were told to focus on passing, moving without the ball and rebounding. All are very simplistic aspects in the game of basketball.

It worked. Indiana won its first seven conference games and was one game away from Coach Tom Crean's longest winning streak at IU. They were also one game away from the team's longest winning streak since Bob Knight left in 2000. Coach Crean listed simplicity as the largest reason for their success.

That's great for IU, obviously, but what's this mean for financial professionals like us? Too often, we complicate our business. We try to emulate the success of businesses or teams who have won lately. It doesn't work. However, time and time again, we find success when we get back to basics.

In any business, "blocking and tackling" won't make the highlight reel, but I assure you those smaller victories will garner success. Take a few minutes and ask yourself, "Am I executing on the basics that drive the core revenues for my business?" If not, it's time to change your game plan.

Winning Strategy: Simplicity wins – in basketball and business.

Always Room to Improve
March 17, 2016

One of the great motivators of our time is Mike Krzyzewski, head men's basketball coach at Duke University. Not only is he a great tactician, but he also teaches his players and assistant coaches many life lessons. Recently, I stumbled on a repeat episode of his Sirius XM radio show. His comments made me think.

At the time of the recording, the Blue Devils had just come off a three-game losing streak – a losing streak is unheard of with Duke basketball – but, Coach K remained positive. He pointed out how they still had a lot going for them:

- His teams had more national championships than losing streaks
- All three losses were by one possession, and not all of them were the last possession
- They had great players and his staff was excellent
- Though most coaches wouldn't be able to eat during a losing streak like this, he really didn't have anything to complain about

So, instead of being down and angry with his team (as many coaches would have been), he encouraged the assistant coaches to think about some little area where they could improve, then use that improvement to better the team. "There is always somewhere to improve," Coach K emphasized. He challenged everyone to look at their body of work and find a spot where they could get better – even in the slightest way.

Improving Your Practice

Using Coach K's methodology, we always have room to improve as financial professionals. In the coming months, the fiduciary standard will force us to look at our business differently. We will all have to look at ourselves and ask the same question: "Where can I improve?"

Best interest standards will mean that we must look at things we might not have considered in the past, or collaborate with other professionals who possess the expertise to fulfill a client need. At the end of the day, we are fortunate to be in this business. Just like Coach K's teams had more success than not, there are so many positives to the financial services profession.

In the same light, there will always be room for us to improve. I'm looking forward to looking in the mirror and improving with the fiduciary standards.

Winning Strategy: There is always room for improvement. Coach K turned a perceived negative into a positive for his team. Use the pending fiduciary standards to make improvements in your business and enhance the client experience.

Are You Asking the Right Question?

March 24, 2016

Have you seen the TV commercial where a client asks her financial advisor some questions? The advertisement focuses on consumers asking better questions. To that point, advisors need to ask better questions, too.

I often hear advisors ask our sales people, "What's the highest or best income rider you have?" But, maybe the better question is:

"What's the highest income I can get my client over their entire lifetime?"

Longevity remains the largest retirement risk – and the greatest multiplier of other risks. It should be every advisor's goal to make sure Americans have a portion of their income (beyond the income provided by government entitlement programs) guaranteed for the remainder of their lives.

With longevity comes retirees' second largest risk, inflation. We have to help clients keep pace with rising costs. Because the longer they live, the more expensive it will be to maintain their standard of living. Without precautions, inflation may eventually erode their ability to buy things 20 years from now that they could easily afford when they first retired.

So, instead of looking at which income rider provides the highest guarantee, we should be focusing on the overall income received throughout retirement. It's easy to get sucked into looking at illustrations and competitor comparisons. However, we need to have a deeper conversation with our clients about their true risks in retirement.

Few Americans really think about how they'll manage their finances 20 years from now – it's our duty to think about that for them. Just like the TV commercial makes consumers rethink their questions, we have to ask better questions, too. We need to think about retirement in its entirety, not just the first year or two.

Winning Strategy: Don't ask about the highest retirement income possible; ask about how you can help clients achieve the highest income over their lifetime. They'll appreciate a longer term focus.

The 3 Traits You Need to be a Leader
March 31, 2016

In a recent post, I mentioned I had the pleasure of listening to Robbie Bach, the former president of entertainment and devices at Microsoft, speak at a meeting. As an accomplished leader, he provided several key points that translate to any business, including financial services. In addition to his thoughts on innovation, he describe three key traits to being an effective leader.

1. **Self-awareness.** In order to be successful, you not only need to have high self-awareness of your own strengths and weaknesses, but also the strengths and weaknesses of your team. For example, during my freshman year at Indiana University, the basketball team had a 7'2" center. Being so tall, he was not good at dribbling the ball to the basket. His best move was a hook shot or a short turnaround jumper. So, we scored quicker and easier when we gave him the ball in the right location on the floor. He was self-aware of his limitations, and his teammates also knew where he could help them win.

2. **Humility.** I think most financial professionals work with a great deal of humility. In a service industry, you have to be thinking of your clients, knowing that without their trust, you wouldn't have a business. In a lot of cases, we reinvest in our own communities through volunteer work or monetary investments. We know we can't be successful without keeping others in the front our mind.

3. **Grit.** Grit isn't easy to define. You might classify it as mental toughness, competitiveness, a willingness to improve or something else along those lines. Essentially, at some point we all must dig deep and believe that all the things we are doing will get us past the difficult times in business. Some people have financial issues, while others might have mental roadblocks. Whatever your obstacle, you must determine the path that will correct the problem and work toward the goal, knowing you will reach it – maybe not as quickly as you'd like, but eventually if you have enough grit.

Leveraging your strengths and making your clients feel important are both critical to long-term success. And, you'll need determination to stick to it and get through the rough times. I hope you remain self-aware and humble, and develop grit along the way.

Winning Strategy: Having self-awareness, humility and grit are critical factors to being an effective, successful leader.

Developing Grit
April 7, 2016

In my previous blog, I described the three traits of leadership, one of which is grit. As I said, grit is always difficult to define. Some consider it perseverance, faith, mental toughness, competitiveness, etc. Personally, I think you develop grit by not only having faith in the outcome, but also by doing the work necessary – repeatedly and consistently.

Grit for the Game

In 1987, I witnessed the development – and fantastic outcome – of grit as a student manager on the Indiana University men's basketball team. Our season ended in a national championship, and the words "Teamwork" and "Toughness" rest on each side of our rings. But, perhaps grit is another word that should be there.

I don't believe our grit was formed in the NCAA tournament when we came from behind in five of our six games – I think it came from an entire season of preparation.

The day and a half leading up to the national championship was the same as we had prepared for every other game. The team saw successful offensive and defensive possessions from Syracuse. There were summaries of each player's tendencies in the locker room. We went to the shoot-around and pre-game meal at exactly the same time and in exactly the same fashion. At tipoff, there was no nervousness. Even though it was the biggest game we'd ever played, we had replicated everything we'd done to be successful before.

We won the championship on our final possession. The most successful aspect of that play was that we ran our normal offense. We didn't get the ball to our All-American shooter like we'd hoped, but that wasn't a problem – our team had run this offense thousands of times before, and someone else got the shot. It was preparation, plain and simple, but people saw resolve and grit to come back and win.

Looking back, I see winning did take grit. However, that grit came from hours of repetition and preparation.

Grit for Your Business

We know 2016 will be a year of transition for many of us financial services professionals, due to the U.S. Department of Labor (DOL) fiduciary standards and conflict of interest rules. We MUST start preparing now so we can develop the grit we need to deal with the post-DOL world of financial services.

Preparing means you need to document your processes and align yourself with organizations that can provide you the best opportunity for success. Those organizations will remain agnostic in their solutions, provide ease of business for you and your clients, and develop the necessary tools to meet the changing needs for our profession.

Winning Strategy: Grit is developed through a high probability of outcomes because you have prepared and done the work you needed to do – repeatedly and consistently. In order to grow your business in 2016 and beyond, you need organizations with the same philosophy around you.

Winning the Same Way Every Time
April 14, 2016

As a student manager for the men's basketball team at Indiana University, I was fortunate to sit at the end of the bench for the 1987 NCAA National Championship. Many people ask me how Coach Bob Knight prepared the team for the final game against Syracuse in the day and half after we beat UNLV in the national semifinals. Well, we did the exact same thing we had done all year.

You see, success follows process and procedure, which eventually allows a team (or business owner) to use their talents effectively. That Final Four run proved that when you follow the successful process you've established, you can relax and play the game freely and confidently.

As we approach a fiduciary standard later in 2016, it's important to set up wining processes now. Following an established process every time will allow you to focus in on the client while acting in their best interest. Pay attention to how you interact with your clients in the following ways:

Engagement – Make sure you have a set routine for each client to explain your services, set expectations and sign a standard engagement letter. The engagement letter (contract) should provide flexibility in how you provide solutions and receive compensation. It's too early in the financial planning process to determine which solutions you'll use or if/how you will receive commissions.

Discovery Process – In order to act in the client's best interest, it's critical to uncover all the necessary information through an established discovery process. Create a written fact finder to document the answers, and be sure they aren't completely quantitative. It's just as important to understand how a client feels and prioritizes their goals is as it is to know their net worth, disposable income and assets.

Analysis – You should leverage a consistent software or set of software tools in your analysis of each case. Having a process that provides dependable output gives you, and the client, assurance they are receiving the best advice.

Presentation – Because you are familiar with the software output, your client presentation should be methodical and factual while emphasizing the key areas of concern. Obviously, this is where you begin to recommend and offer solutions. If you have followed your standard process up to this point and have established their needs, how you receive compensation will likely be irrelevant to the client.

Implementation and Review – One of the most frustrating things clients tell us is that their financial professional failed to follow up on the plan. It's really important to make sure all your recommendations were executed – either by you or another financial professional – and that you take the initiative to make sure all those recommendations are performing properly and still meet the client's goals.

Many financial professionals remain concerned about the pending fiduciary standards. However, I argue the vast majority of our sales professionals are following some sort of established process already.

Instead of worrying about changing your financial planning practice on a dime, look to review and refine your established processes. Make sure they are agnostic to companies and compensation. Most importantly, write those processes down so that you have documentation in the event you are challenged by a client in the future. Following the same processes over and over will give you the same confidence the Hoosiers had playing in the national championship game.

Winning Strategy: Establish and follow your selling process for success. Having set standards allows you to focus on the client and meet or exceed their expectations.

How Flexibility Will Help You Win the Game
April 21, 2016

During mega sporting events like the Super Bowl, quite often you hear the word resiliency. But, I think few people really know what it takes to be resilient.

Too often, people think you reach success by "pounding away" like the Carolina Panthers on the road to Super Bowl 50. Without a doubt, the franchise made a great run in the 2015-16 season by continuing to pound, but they were defeated by a team that showed flexibility.

When you look up the definition of resiliency, it mentions "having elasticity." Not surprisingly, the Denver Broncos, who defeated the Panthers in the Super Bowl, displayed elasticity throughout the season. Specifically, quarterback Peyton Manning became more flexible and elastic in his management of the game.

The Struggle
Starting the season, the Broncos were a favorite to win the Super Bowl. But, as many football seasons do, the next 17 weeks were filled with promise, disappointment, concern and eventually, frustration. Many teams would have allowed those circumstances to define their season. Peyton was injured and sat on the bench for several weeks. He watched how the backup succeeded and learned the true strength of

their team was their defense. He didn't have to win every game; he just didn't have to lose.

The Opportunity

In the playoffs, Peyton's performance was clearly not the same as it had been in the previous two decades of his career. However, he managed the game to the best of his ability and recognized what he could do and couldn't do.

The Payoff

During the Super Bowl, he didn't seem to force anything. Instead, he paid attention to what the defense provided him, and he capitalized on it. I'm sure he would have liked to have thrown a bunch of touchdowns and set records, but it wasn't good for the team. He was resilient in his game plan because he was able to change and adapt in a high pressure situation.

My point? Resiliency isn't about "keeping your nose to the grindstone." Flexibility allows you to recognize opportunity, which is just as important as reaching a previously set goal. Sometimes you have to give up aspects of your original vision in order to reach a higher level in your game.

Winning Strategy: True resiliency in business is the ability to adapt to change and maneuver around disruption. Be flexible instead of rock hard in your determination to succeed.

How to Position Yourself for Opportunity
April 28, 2016

At Indiana University, Coach Bob Knight's rules of defense were mostly based on being able to recognize the situation. Players had to always be aware of what was happening on the court – just like we must always be aware of what's happening in our businesses.

The Ball-You-Man rule means you stay between the ball and the player you're guarding. You may think it would be easy to stay close to your man, but that isn't effective – you'll just do a lot of extra running around to chase him down. Instead, you want to stay closer to the ball so you can help support your teammates.

If the ball is on the opposite side of the court from your man, you want to stay on the same side as the ball, keeping your man in peripheral vision. If the ball swings over to the top of the court or to your man's side, you can immediately try to deny the pass. Everyone on defense must be constantly moving and adjusting their position, looking for any opportunity to get the ball back.

Defense for Your Business

In financial services, each client represents a new possession. We must react to their unique needs and objectives. More importantly, we must move to different positions as their goals change throughout their life's journey.

Looking at the bigger picture, we have to recognize any opportunities the new fiduciary rules will provide us. Yes, the rules will force us to change our practices, but those of us who can recognize and react before the ball arrives will succeed in making the transition.

You can defend your business by taking some basic steps:

- Create written policies and procedures – this will provide protection against possible litigation by showing you follow a documented process that leads to agnostic solutions and client-centered recommendations
- Have a partner with providers that remain independent of conflict, allowing you to find financial recommendations that are in the best interests of your clients without regard to carrier-specific incentives
- Do what you're likely already doing: Delivering education and advice that's built on trust and expertise – if you do that, the compensation won't matter

These things might be adjustments to what you're doing in your financial practice today. But, moving before the ball moves will place you in a better position to win. The pending rules will open the door to many opportunities that our industry can capitalize on … as long as we're in the right position.

Winning Strategy: Good defense requires you to recognize the situation on the court and place yourself in the right position. Make sure your business is in the right position for the fiduciary standards of the future.

Part II

Sales Motivation

Thoughts from Others

Top of the Mountain

By Ryan McGee - August 20, 2015

Standing at the edge of Erickson Bowl, elevation 12,480, in Keystone, Colorado, I was in awe. As I looked out on the summit at Keystone Peak, searching for a line to begin my descent down the snow-covered mountain, the sunlight was blinding. I noticed the fresh smell of minty pine, and the view of pristine blue skies and crystal white snow took my breath away.

This is was a place of tranquility, but the atmosphere shifted quickly and the piercing cold wind was a shock to my face. I'd made the steep journey to the summit, but I stood there frightened about the possibilities of the suicide mission to return.

As I flew down at 60 miles an hour, I had to trust my equipment, my knowledge of the terrain and my technical skills. I veered right and left, avoiding trees and boulders that could potentially kill me in a second. It was a thrill, but a very risky thrill, and I couldn't have done it without preparation.

Right now, your clients are at the mountaintop of a six-year bull market and volatility has returned. They may feel uncertain and unprepared for the potential risks they face – inflation, health care and outliving their money. Do you know how to guide them through the terrain to safety?

Winning Strategy: You can enjoy the view from the top … but eventually, you'll have to head back down from the summit. Help your clients mitigate risks and successfully navigate the retirement mountain. It's quite a thrill.

Practice Makes Perfect

By Steve Schankerman - August 6, 2015

My seventh-grade son played his first season of middle school basketball this year. To be honest, he didn't play well and didn't get as much playing time as he'd hoped. Instead of being discouraged, however, he continued to work hard and practice.

It's paid off. He's improved dramatically over the last month, and he's getting much more playing time with his summer team. It's a great jump-start for him because his summer coach will also be his eighth-grade coach next year.

With the large amount of baby boomers retiring over the next few years, it seems like the financial industry is also starting a new season, too. Advisors need to be focused on retirement income planning, but it will take a lot of work and practice to stand out in the crowd.

Winning Strategy: If you want to help your clients win, you need to be a good coach. With hard work and practice, you can be your clients' go-to resource for retirement income planning.

The Real Retirement Fears

By Bill Stutz - August 27, 2015

I think baby boomers are starting to get the message (at least at the conceptual level) of the need and costs of addressing longevity in retirement. Just watch 60 minutes of primetime network TV – you'll see green lines, orange money, falling dominoes and some scolding from Tommy Lee Jones. See, you know exactly what I am talking about without me even mentioning the sponsors of those commercials.

If retirement planning were only that simple ...

If longevity was the only risk to going broke in retirement, your job would be easy. But, it's not. Effective retirement planning requires getting inside your clients' heads and hearts and learning their fears and concerns about what could cause them to run out of money.

Concerns that fueled their fear of going broke in retirement include:

- Health care costs - 76%
- Market fluctuations - 62%
- Lifestyle expenses - 52%
- Unexpected costs - 46%
- Being a financial burden - 24%
- Desire to leave an inheritance - 21%
- Financial support of children - 12%

As a financial professional, one the biggest challenges you face is helping clients articulate and identify their individual retirement concerns. Might I suggest using the above list to jump-start the conversation?

Winning Strategy: In order to address your clients' retirement worries, you have to dig deeper than the numbers. Find out what potentially troubling events concern them most – then find solutions to help calm their fears.

Q1 2015 AICPA CPA Personal Financial Planning Trends Survey.

Annuities: A Top Pick

By Jason Caudill - January 12, 2015

The nature of my job dictates that I spend a lot of time in my car. When I'm driving, I'm typically either talking on my phone or listening to sports radio on ESPN. Not too long ago, one of my favorite sports show hosts was talking about the NFL draft and how difficult it is for franchises to select the best possible college player for their top draft pick. In college football, there's an abundance of talented athletes who look very promising; however, it's almost impossible to know for sure if their talent will translate into success in the NFL.

The commenter said selecting a draft pick is exactly like selecting a financial advisor: Regardless of who your advisor is, you would've made money over the last two years ... You won't know if you have a great advisor until you see what they do in a difficult environment.

Consider this: On Jan. 5, 2015, the S&P 500 closed at $2,020.58, and just two years ago on Jan. 4, 2013, the S&P 500 closed at $1,466.67 – the index is up 38 percent and near an all-time high.

Despite all the market success, all the studies we're seeing point toward the fact that many near-retirees are ready to take some of their "winnings" off the table and "lock in" their gains.

We need to spread the word: Indexed annuities are an attractive option today with more, and better, features than they've ever had before. As you're sitting with your clients, reviewing their portfolios' performance this past year, ask about their sentiments of the equity market moving forward, and broach the subject of locking in a portion of their gains.

Winning Strategy: Show your clients that you can help them succeed in a difficult environment ... show them you won't disappoint them as their top draft pick.

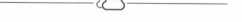

The Risky Business of Life

By Jason Caudill - July 30, 2015

Seemingly everything we do as part of our normal daily lives has some level of risk. We make decisions every day to help mitigate our level of risk; some of these decisions are even done subconsciously or purely out of habit.

Some activities in our daily routines have a risk associated with them, whether we know it or not. For instance, how many of you have ever read the back of your toothpaste tube? I decided to read mine this morning and found, "Warning: If more than used for brushing is accidentally swallowed, get medical help or contact a poison control center right away." Who knew using too much toothpaste was a risk?!

Many risks are viewed differently today than they were 20 years ago, and I would say, as a society, we have become much more risk averse. When I was a kid, my father had a two-door pickup truck with a cover on the back of it. Occasionally on the weekends, he and my mom would put all our bicycles in the back of the truck and take us to the park to ride around the pond. The part I remember being most fun is all three of us kids riding in the back of the truck. Today, I would venture to say there are very few who would attempt this stunt, and if someone did, they would get plenty of dirty looks.

Although smoking cigarettes has become taboo and organic food is the new vogue, many Americans still take unnecessary risks with their investments. While we have had an amazing bull market and are achieving new all-time highs since the lows in March of 2009, there are certainly still risks when investing in equities.

Winning Strategy: At a time when we are becoming more conservative as a society, many people are becoming less risk averse with money; perhaps simply because they are not aware of any good options that eliminate or reduce risk.

Avoid That Difficult Conversation

By John Duchien - October 1, 2015

Think back over your career in financial services. Of the thousands of conversations you've had with your clients over the years, think of the most difficult ones – the ones that, even now, give you that queasy feeling in your stomach as you recall the circumstances.

When I ask advisors to describe their most difficult conversation, each answer is slightly unique, based on their particular situations, but almost all fall into a few categories:

- Market losses (stocks, bonds, mutual funds, variable annuities)
- Income shortfall at retirement
- Estate erosion upon a disability or long-term care event

- Not having enough life insurance upon the death of a client

In virtually every case, the advisor freely admits the blame rests largely with him or her. They know things could have been different if they were a bit more adamant about covering the specific needs and risk tolerances of their clients, and positioning them to handle any eventuality.

As the conversation continues, my next logical question is, "So, what are you doing now to make sure you avoid having to have a similar difficult conversation in the future?"

Winning Strategy: Look at solutions to help your clients avoid the perils of market volatility, income shortfall, catastrophic injury or illness, or premature death. Your client conversations down the road will be much more pleasant.

Training for the Marathon of Retirement
By Bentley Heese - October 15, 2015

Long distance running can actually be enjoyable. There, I said it, and I'm standing behind it. I really enjoy the training process of preparing for an event, whether it's a half marathon (13.1 miles), a marathon (26.2 miles) and yes, even an ultra-marathon (any distance greater than 26.2 miles).

I was never an athlete growing up, but I've observed that most people who don't like running participated in other sports where running was viewed as punishment. In reality, it is a great foundation for the endurance required to excel in most other sports.

The training process for all distances is extremely important for success, and I feel retirement income planning should be approached in the same manner. Would you wake up one day and just decide to go out and run 26.2 miles? I didn't think so. Most training plans last four to six months leading up to the event, depending on your level of fitness prior to starting. Sticking to the plan as much as possible is imperative – if you cannot commit to 90 percent or more of the plan you've laid out, your likelihood of finishing reduces dramatically. It's a steady process that builds your base fitness over the training cycle, then tapers off before the race to allow your body to rest and prepare.

When planning for retirement income, you build your base, stay the course in terms of your personal risk index and then "taper" five to 10 years out. A marathon is 26.2 miles, but your retirement will possibly last even longer than that in terms of years. Are you just going to wake up one day and start that journey of retirement? I hope not, otherwise your chances of success will be nominal at best. You must build a strong foundation you can customize for income, health care and longevity.

Winning Strategy: A marathon is tough, but like longevity, preparation is the key so you don't hit that "wall" at mile 20.

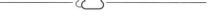

Be Ready for Change
By Jeff Hood - November 12, 2015

Change. Wow, some things sure have changed in the insurance business, while others remain the same. (More about that in a bit.)

At the risk of showing my age, I remember selling life insurance out of a rate book. Paper illustrations were next, and now we can display values on an iPad or other mobile device. The same goes with mutual fund sales – they used to include a paper prospectus. Now, a CD delivers the same information.

I just attended our national sales meeting and change was a continuous topic. The message was loud and clear: Be prepared and able to change because change is constant.

The market is always introducing new products, and new strategies to use them. Government regulations and carrier changes can make our jobs more complex, but they can also make things more interesting.

Don't forget our clients' needs are always evolving, too. Retirement planning isn't what it used to be, and the economy can change without notice. We have to be on our toes if we want to be effective.

That brings me back to my opening sentence … There are some constants in our business, such as protection and reliability. Clients will always need solutions to give them those things … and they'll always need professionals like us to deliver them!

Winning Strategy: Be ready for change, but hold on to your beliefs for the solutions we provide. The core of our business will never change.

Never Too Late to Win
By Jeff Hood - February 13, 2015

Born and raised in Indiana, I, like many Hoosiers, came to love the game of basketball. In 1995, the New York Knicks were playing my Indiana Pacers in game one of the eastern conference semi-finals, and I can recall when one of the most spectacular 18.7 seconds left in the game unfolded. Reggie Miller, a shooting guard for Indiana, scored 8 points in 11 seconds and sealed the victory for the Pacers. If you're a fan of the sport, you have to see it – if you haven't already, Google Reggie Miller to watch this unlikely feat.

I share this great moment in sports history to remind everyone it's never too late. Clients nearing or in retirement can still protect their savings – for themselves, and potentially for their beneficiaries! There are countless strategies to lean on, and not enough space or time to begin to reference them all. With that said, there are three common-sense ideas that are widely recommended by financial advisors across the country.

1. **Be ready for the next market correction.** Since 1957, there has been a market correction (a loss of 10 percent or greater) about every two years on average. The last correction was in the summer months of 2011, when the S&P 500 fell 19 percent. The lesson here is to make sure your asset allocation is up to date based on a current risk tolerance model, and maximize safety in your investments.

2. **Make certain you have a strategy in place for guaranteed lifetime income.** Remember, survey after survey suggests that running out of money is the No. 1 concern of seniors today. Fixed indexed annuities with lifetime income riders put the

"guarantee" in guaranteed lifetime income.

3. **If your clients plan on leaving some assets to their beneficiaries, they should consider buying life insurance, especially if those assets are qualified.** The tax-free death benefit for your beneficiaries will help offset tax due on the passing of those qualified assets at your death.

Winning Strategy: Reggie Miller knew it was never too late to win the game. Employ some common-sense strategies today, and it won't be too late for your clients, either!

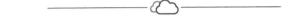

Be a 'Go-Giver' and You'll Come Out Ahead

By Randy Kitzmiller - September 17, 2015

I am not an avid reader. But last winter, my wife received a book called "The Go-Giver," by Bob Burg and John David Mann.

I sat down thinking I would only read about one chapter, lose interest, and put the book on my bookshelf to collect dust. Interestingly enough, two hours later I was finished with the book. I was so enamored with it; I sat down and read it again the next day. I was even so inspired that I bought 50 copies to give to some of my top advisors.

I'm not here to give you a book report because I'd like you to actually read this book yourself. But the message is this: Your income is determined by how well you serve others. In an instant gratification society, we are so caught up with, "What is in this for me?" We don't realize the value we bring to others will take care of us for our lifetimes.

The best example of this is a conversation I had with Jim Ash, the founder of Ash Brokerage. We had a prospective group of advisors – a large opportunity – in our offices in Fort Wayne, and we took them to dinner. Jim discussed with them how we were able to land a few of our larger accounts.

One example was a large mutual insurance company for which we were going to be a brokerage outlet if they could not place cases with their career company. After a couple of months, the GAs of this firm had a huge increase in their OWN product line. When they questioned the advisors about what they were doing differently, they said, "Ash Brokerage is giving us positioning ideas on our own product line." That being said, there was no instant gratification for Ash Brokerage, but this is now one of our largest accounts.

I also know a peer who is a very successful wholesaler in a different product line, and he prides himself on knowing every product available. When one doesn't fit, he always recommends one that will. Needless to say, he's now in upper management at his firm, running the top territory in his company.

Winning Strategy: Your income is always dependent on how well you serve others. If you just do the right things in life, even if there is no instant gratification, you'll come out ahead.

Sometimes, You Just Know

By Dan Lavigne - June 25, 2015

Twenty-two years ago, I was a finance major at the University of Idaho, where I was studying modern portfolio theory and managed a small portfolio for the university's business school. We utilized multiple securities analysis techniques, as well a piece of software – which only the University of Idaho and Stanford University were allowed to use – to construct the portfolio.

I knew the research we had done for that portfolio would pay off, and I realized we were on the leading edge of great advances in construction. There are just times in life when you, "just know."

It was years before I saw anything in the marketplace that constructed portfolios any more efficiently or effectively than we did at that time. Today, you can find more powerful tools on just about any financial site you visit. In fact, the accumulation side of this business has become so seemingly commoditized we now have robo-advice, which is nearly indistinguishable from much of the human advice.

For years now, I've been studying the decummulation side of

portfolio construction, and once again in my life I feel like I, "just know." I'm working with a team who's on the edge of great portfolio construction; only this time, it's for the back nine of life.

Most advisors, as well as many clients, have heard about the risks of retirement, yet portfolios continue to be constructed as if those risks were some kind of old wives' tale. If you and your clients have figured out a way to minimize sequence of returns risk, inoculate against interest rate risk and volatility risk, and have eliminated longevity risk, all while keeping tax efficiencies and Social Security maximization in mind, then we will be of little help to you.

On the other hand, if you would like to have a team to bounce ideas off of, or actually help construct portfolios like these, then we're going to have an incredible solution.

Winning Strategy: This business has become too complicated for any one person to be an expert in all areas and still have time to take care of clients. If you're not prepared to help with the decummulation risks of your clients' retirement portfolio, find someone who can.

What if These are 'The Good Old Days'?

By Jim Martin - October 8, 2015

If you knew "the good old days" were happening right now, what would you do differently? What would you eat, buy or do more of? Which opportunities – that maybe you didn't take advantage of or took partial advantage of – would you want to seize so you don't look back in regret?

I'm not talking about stopping to smell the roses, though that's never a bad idea. But, isn't it true that we tend to isolate and romanticize things from the past, blocking out a preponderance of other, negative things that were going on at the same time? Whether it was "the good old days" of more respectful youth (Vietnam), "Leave it to Beaver" middle class America (a martini and cigarette for dessert) or the days of the "perfect President" (pick one – the rose colored glasses of either party are equally myopic and revisionist), the "reality" of the past is really in our interpretation of it. In planning our financial futures, it is equally as dangerous to look fondly on the past as it is to look optimistically to the future. We need to focus on the now! We've been told that interest rates would be rising for at least the last five years. How many earnings have been lost waiting for that to happen? And how much more will continue to be lost, waiting until that magic percentage rate is reached?

Alternatives exist now to participate in the market's current positive trajectory, lock in gains and providing future flexibility. Not acting now could result in retirement savings disappearing and becoming a bitter memory as the result of an upcoming market correction.

Here's the trap: Now may not seem like a good time to take action because you are too busy, you have other more urgent things to do, interest rates are too low, there's an election coming up, etc. Later seems better because you (think you) will have more time, more money, more information and better opportunities.

Winning Strategy: Will later be better? Or will later turn out to be the worst of times – too late? Take action now. Give yourself the chance to look back and say, "Those were the good old days."

Uncovering New Sales
By John Duchien - August 7, 2014

I'm often asked where advisors are finding client funds for fixed and indexed annuities in our current economic environment. In my opinion, most annuity sales are coming from three sources: equities, banks or bonds.

As financial markets reflect increasing volatility, more and more advisors are suggesting clients take some of their gains from the last few years off the table. Clients are increasingly open to the idea of protecting their gains by moving some of their equity assets into guaranteed products, such as fixed and indexed annuities. Investors who, during the past 14 years, patiently stayed in the market through two severe corrections, are anxious to protect themselves against another potential downturn.

I think banks are the most obvious source of annuity funding. With consumer deposit rates hovering at historic lows for more than five years, clients who've been waiting for higher rates are running out of patience. The quest for a higher return without principal fluctuation risk lends itself naturally to fixed and indexed annuities.

In bonds and bond funds, there's an entire generation of investors who've never experienced a prolonged bear market. As advisors are looking at their clients' asset allocations, many are looking for bond and bond fund alternatives that are not subject to principal deterioration if rates start to rise. Again, fixed and indexed annuities are often the best solution.

Winning Strategy: You should take a fresh look at your practice's current client files. Chances are, annuity sales are waiting to be uncovered.

Summer's Almost Gone …
But Opportunities Remain

By Bentley Heese - September 7, 2014

Throughout the summer, we've shared information and ideas on the complacency bubble, opportunity cost (otherwise referred to as cost of waiting), clients in transition, income generation and a plethora of other topics to encourage you to change your behavior, along with your clients' behavior. We think we've presented some compelling ideas and data that have the potential to enhance your financial practice and help you manage client expectations.

Throughout our dialogue, the market has continued to march upward, unabated by developing domestic and global issues. It seems almost unstoppable, but we know it can't continue this trend indefinitely. Many advisors continue to choose the path of least resistance, and we see huge amounts of inflows continuing weekly into mutual funds, equities and bonds. I encourage you to keep positioning annuities for some of your clients where appropriate.

Though there are many client scenarios for which you should consider using annuities, here are four prevailing ones that you'll likely encounter:

1. **Clients in your book of business who are over age 59 ½ and still working:** Discuss in-service withdrawals with them

2. **Clients within five years of retirement who are still fully invested in the market:** Think about starting to lock in those returns with an indexed annuity

3. **Clients who have part of the $10 trillion sitting on the sidelines, waiting for advice:** Consider alternatives such as single-premium deferred annuities or fixed index annuities

4. **Clients who have portfolios in need of risk reduction:** Possibly reduce exposure to interest rate risk with a fixed index annuity

Winning Strategy: As we ramp back up from summer mode into what is generally the best third of the year, think about the kind of advisor you want to be. Are you the one who makes it happen, the one who lets it happen, or the one who says, "What happened?"

Sales and Customer Service

By Jeff Hood - November 24, 2014

For most of my life, my father was an executive with Sears-Roebuck. One of his favorite sayings was, "We are a sales organization; nothing happens until something is sold." Truer words were never spoken, and if you are a financial advisor, those words resonate loud and clear.

The process and resulting sale made by a financial advisor is much different than selling a washing machine or a refrigerator. While these sales are transactional in nature, the decision to purchase an annuity or life insurance policy is based by and large on the strength of the relationship between the advisor and the client.

Regardless, making a sale in our business is imperative to survival. But, what happens after the sale might very well distinguish you as an advisor, build and strengthen the relationship, and create easy referrals.

Here are the magic words: customer service. Your clients are craving it! So, how can we offer exceptional customer service?

- Make sure you are scheduling annual checkups – these are a perfect opportunity to be front and center
- Have your client's favorite drink ready for them, and ask about their family and hobbies
- Between appointments, send articles and information that might be helpful to them (remember, they can get information online all day – information directly from someone they trust is different)
- Send a birthday card or any other card you feel is appropriate – just remember to write a little note and sign it personally

These are just ideas to get started. I'm sure there are many more ways to provide great customer service.

Winning Strategy: I would agree with my dad: Nothing happens until something is sold … but great customer service happens after the sale!

Trust and Reputation

By Jeff Hood - September 2, 2014

Professionals have advice for everything, it seems. In the game of golf, they tell you to keep your head down. In real estate, it's all about "location, location, location."

In sales, trust and reputation are key to not only creating new relationships and helping new clients, but also in maintaining your current book of business.

As an insurance producer, how does trust and reputation help you find new clients? Well, primarily by referrals. Successful producers are trusted and own a good reputation, therefore their clients may be more inclined to recommend them to other people.

But what about your current clients? As their advisor, you can build even more trust, and grow your reputation by making annual policy reviews a must-do in your practice. What are the advantages of annual reviews?

- Identifying any new client goals
- Reviewing beneficiaries to ensure accuracy
- Looking for life-changing events that may change their needs and/or contract
- Reviewing performance of current contracts
- Implementing any reallocations
- Reviewing lifetime income goals
- Creating referrals

I am certain there are many more reasons to include annual reviews in your practice, and I would like to include one more: You will likely surpass your clients' expectations by showing them that you really do care. You will increase your persistence, and will grow your reputation and trust in your community.

Winning Strategy: Remember, head down in golf, location in real estate, and trust and reputation in sales!

Encouragement in Today's Environment

By Ryan McGee - June 20, 2014

State of the Nation: Your success is not contingent on a product or a rate!

Sometimes, as advisors, we can become discouraged with market conditions, especially when our livelihoods could be disrupted by things out of our control. As we continue to see a significant number of pricing decreases from carriers, along with the pressures of our current rate environment, you might be wondering how to keep these challenges in perspective.

First, don't buy into the mindset that guaranteed products are no longer competitive. Your clients still need your help and expertise to provide better, safe returns on their money. Our solutions remain one of the best alternatives for clients seeking safety, higher rates of return and guaranteed income. According to bankrate.com, there is still a large amount of funds – $13 trillion – earning less than 25 basis points in banks and institutions. And, as of last week, the national average for a five-year CD was .79 percent.[1]

Recently released numbers from the LIMRA Secure Retirement Institute show total annuity sales improved 11 percent in the first quarter of 2014, compared to the first quarter of 2013, totaling $57.7 billion. [2]

According to the report, the sales were driven largely by fixed annuities, which experienced a 43 percent increase in the first quarter, reaching $23.5 billion. Indexed annuity sales also rose 43 percent in the first quarter, totaling $11.3 billion.

This proves the opportunity is there, and clients are responding!

Winning Strategy: To help your clients succeed, I truly believe the stars are aligned between the intersection of opportunity and strategic partnership. You should take advantage of both.

[1]*Bankrate.com as of June 2014.*
[2] *"LIMRA Secure Retirement Institute: Total Annuity Sales Increase by 11 Percent in First Quarter," May 2014.*

Goldilocks and the Split Ticket: A Retirement Tale

By Steve Schankerman - November 3, 2014

Goldilocks tried three different porridge bowls before finding one that was, "just right." When choosing where to draw income during retirement, the markets offer similar options: too hot, too cold and just right.

If your client chooses just one annuity – variable or fixed indexed – market performance can make their selection either too hot or too cold. However, by positioning your clients with a split ticket – a combination of the two annuities – you give them options for withdrawing income from one or the other. Depending on market performance, they'll be able to use the option that's just right!

Here's how it works: If the equity markets are performing well, the last thing an investor should do is drain their "bowl." Variable annuities with guaranteed income riders can ratchet up their income base with each market advancement. Therefore, income should be taken from fixed index annuities.

If the markets break even or are declining, it's not likely that the account value will ever push the income base higher than the guaranteed growth of the index annuity (especially with the internal costs of a variable annuity being around 4 percent). In this situation, income should absolutely be taken from the variable annuity.

Winning Strategy: The concept of a split ticket has probably been around as long as "Goldilocks and the Three Bears." With the movement of baby boomers into retirement, this concept should definitely be revisited.

Don't Blink

By Michael Senkier - July 1, 2014

Don't blink ... time is flying by!

June was Annuity Awareness Month, and we have completed the first half of 2014. Wow, where has the time gone? We have seen the markets roller-coastering and the bond market bouncing around. The S&P is up around 6.2 percent and the 10-year treasury started at 3 percent and has been floating around the 2.6 percent range before hitting a low of 2.4 percent.

This a great time to step back and look at where we're going. Most of us have kids, grandkids and clients ready to enjoy the summer and head away for some family vacations. What a great time to make sure we have things in order.

You may be asking yourself, "What does it mean to have things in order?" Is it choosing a vacation destination or how we will get there? Or, is it about the car being up to date on maintenance so we can make the trip with ease?

Of course, those things are important. We want to make sure we have things in order before we head off on the road. But, let's give the following financial aspects a second look for our clients, too:

- Do they have beneficiaries listed for all assets? (insurance, 401(k), IRA, annuities or mutual funds)
- Have they protected the ones they care about? (Have we forgotten someone or need to make an adjustment?)
- Have they just been declined for insurance or long-term care? (Illness, results of lab work or family history open a can of worms)
- Is their will up to date and advance medical directive in order?

Things happen in the blink of an eye; it feels like we just started the new year and now it's half over.

Winning Strategy: As you touch base with your clients, or see them before they head off for their next family vacation, remember to ask a few questions to make sure they didn't blink and forget to protect the ones they love most.

Part III

Products

Thoughts from Mike

The Opportunity of Pension Transfers
April 30, 2015

A salesperson often gets asked, "What's the largest case you've ever written?" My answer is always that I haven't written it ... YET. However, that time may be coming soon. Due to changes in the pension environment, I think we should get into position to write large cases in 2016 and 2017.

Significant changes in the pension landscape make it a great time to discuss transferring the plan's risk to an insurance carrier. First, due to the continued bull market, plans have increased in value. February's corporate plan funding index increased to 87.5 percent after posting its best 30-day performance since January 2011.[1]

With plans closer to being fully funded, business owners must write a smaller check to reduce or eliminate the risk from the balance sheet. Along those same lines, rising interest rates in the future will erode the bond valuations of current plans, making it more costly to transfer the risk. Now is the right time to have the conversation.

Second, the Society of Actuaries has suggested – and Congress has approved – the change in actuarial assumptions in pension plans. It is expected that the actuarial changes alone will negatively affect funding levels by as much as 8 percent.[2,3] Due to the length of time it takes to move a plan to a carrier from Department of Labor standards, most plans will likely be affected by this.

Finally, premiums for the Pension Benefit Guaranty Corporation are on the rise, with plans paying $49 per participant in 2014, $57 in 2015 and $64 in 2016. Underfunded plans also pay a variable premium per $1,000 underfunded of $14 in 2014, $24 in 2015 and $29 in 2016.[4] These premiums will increase the overall cost of maintaining a fully funded plan by more than 30 percent and significantly more for underfunded plans.

If you are looking for a way to talk to business owners, and at the same time write a big case, consider exploring the pension termination marketplace. The time is ripe for advisors to bring business owners a solution that is ready to help them in 2016.

Winning Strategy: Look at the pension termination market for the opportunity to write larger cases in 2015 and 2016.

[1]*"Funded Status of U.S. Corporate Pensions Rises Five Percent in February, According to BNY Mellon ISSG," BNY Mellon, March 3, 2015.*
[2]*RP-2014 Mortality Tables, Experience Studies – Pension, Society of Actuaries.*
[3]*Mercer Longevity Insights: Your Industry vs. the General Population," Mercer, December 5, 2014.*
[4]*Pension Benefit Guaranty Corporation, rates as of April 30, 2015.*

Retirement Through Air Travel
January 1, 2015

I fly nearly 60,000 miles per year, and I'm still amazed at the size of the aircraft that manage to take off and stay aloft. But pilots will tell you there are four basic principles that make air travel safe: thrust, lift, weight and drag. I think most Americans can benefit from the same four principles in retirement.

Thrust: Now is the best time to buy a fixed annuity. Given the likelihood of low interest rates for the foreseeable future, an additional 100-150 basis points in rate make a surprising difference in accumulating money. Change your conversation to focus on the time it will take to double your client's money. With today's rates, it can make a 36-year difference – that's thrust in a financial plan.

Lift: One of the basic benefits of an annuity is tax deferral. Over time, tax deferral can make a significant difference in the accumulation value of nonqualified dollars. If nominal interest rates are similar, tax deferral provides lift in retirement planning. Tax considerations need to be evaluated during the distribution phase as well. Life insurance and exclusion ratios can be a tool to ladder income payouts at retirement. Positioning income with respect to taxation also allows clients to maximize their government entitlement programs.

Weight: Weight slows an aircraft down and makes it inefficient, just as investment portfolios become inefficient when their asset classes have not been weighed properly. A diversified strategy to take advantage of all investment options makes returns more stable over long periods of time. Additionally, taking gains off the table allows an investor to reduce the weight of their portfolio. Re-balancing the portfolio regularly keeps the asset allocation in line and allows the client to take gains off the table with more conservative vehicles provides more consistent returns.

Drag: When flying, resistance comes from many items on an aircraft. Reducing drag allows the plane to fly faster and more efficiently. Aside from taxes, fees are one of the biggest drags on an investment portfolio. Whether they're advisory or product fees, they make the portfolio work harder to attain desired results. Client-friendly annuities and life insurance (during both the accumulation and income phases) allow clients to reach their goals faster.

When talking to clients about their retirement goals, try to think about how to keep their retirement portfolio soaring. Provide thrust in the form of better nominal rates; create lift through tax deferral; reduce the weight of equity-heavy portfolios; and minimize the drag in fees.

Winning Strategy: Flying may seem complex, but it can be broken down into four simple principles – use them to make your clients' retirement portfolios soar like an airplane.

The Good News of Market Downturns
November 19, 2015

Many people look at market corrections in largely a negative way. Of course, we can always talk to clients about buying low and selling high as a reason to invest or reinvest when a correction occurs. Just like making lemonade out of lemons, advisors should evaluate all angles of a client's situation and look for ways to improve it in an ever-changing world.

Following the August 2015 market drop, a potentially good subject to bring up at your fourth quarter client meetings is the re-characterization of Roth IRAs. Oct. 15 was the cutoff to change a Roth IRA back to a Traditional IRA for the previous year. However, if your client took advantage of converting a Traditional IRA to a Roth prior to the market dip in 2015, there are reasons to look at re-characterizing the asset back to a Traditional IRA and then re-convert.

Because the client converted prior to the correction, that client will pay taxes on the larger amount converted. Re-characterizing the asset allows them to eliminate the tax consequences at the higher asset value. The asset must stay a Traditional IRA for 30 days; then, the funds can be re-converted to a Roth IRA at the lower market value. Assuming the market stays lower than the original conversion date, the client can convert the same amount of shares at a lower value and less tax. Then, any future gains (even those below the original conversion amount) grow tax-deferred and are accessed tax-free for qualified withdrawals.

Of course, the client only benefits from this transaction if the account value stays below the originally converted amount prior to the re-conversion. This is a market risk you and a client must discuss. However, this tactic allows them to potentially convert more under the same tax bracket than prior to the market correction.

Looking at ways to efficiently convert funds from a taxable consequence during retirement to a tax-free status positions the client for potentially more disposable income later in life, and it gives them a higher probability of not running out of money. That's truly looking out for your client's best interest. When you have that conversation, my guess is your client will appreciate your knowledge and attention to detail in handling their account.

Winning Strategy: Look toward the tax code for opportunities to open up conversations with your client and help position more tax-free income for them later in life.

Do You Know What You Own?

May 7, 2015

Anyone can look at their quarterly statements and see what they have in their portfolio, right? But, do you really know what you own? Granted, you can easily see the ticker symbols for your mutual funds, but you might be surprised to know how much drift there is in any mutual fund in the United States.

It's always good to sit down with your clients and review their portfolio's asset allocation—many advisors use tools such as Morningstar, Albridge or other data aggregates. Before your client meeting, however, it's important to review the style drift and correlation of the selected mutual funds. Style drift happens when fund managers tend to chase returns and look to different asset classes to gain extra return. Before you know it, the large cap equity fund becomes a small cap emerging growth fund.

It's the advisor's responsibility to make sure the fund managers continue to meet the requirements of the allocation strategy by maintaining their expected asset class.

A recent article from Financial Planning highlighted the increased correlation in returns between several bond funds and the S&P 500.[1] Due to the continued low-interest-rate environment, many bond funds perform similar to equities. The idea of an asset allocation strategy is to have uncorrelated assets in the portfolio to balance and reduce volatility. While those bond funds may have maintained the integrity of their portfolio design at one time, the current economic environment makes it necessary to revisit their viability in today's portfolios.

When you dig deep in your clients' portfolios, you're promoting trust and deeper relationships. Take the extra time to review all aspects of the portfolio, including risks and potential solutions to reduce risks. Many of us may not see the risks of our current allocation strategy until it's too late. Take the extra step to look at vehicles that remain uncorrelated to portfolios.

Winning Strategy: The current economic environment has

changed the way traditional investment vehicles perform. Take time to re-evaluate the products used for a client's asset allocation strategy and reduce volatility due to highly correlated investments.

[1] *"Warning: Bond Funds That Act Like Stocks," Financial Planning, January 26, 2015.*

Now is the Best Time to Sell Fixed Annuities!
December 22, 2014

Many may question my sanity when they read the title of this blog. You might think you can't put your client in a fixed account during some of the lowest interest rates in the U.S. history. However, in sales, it is all relative to the current situation, environment and client attitude.

Try positioning the current fixed sale in relation to the impact the current interest rate can have on your client's funds in terms of time. One of our top sales professionals challenges his advisors to change their mindset and look at ways to impact their clients – he uses the Rule of 72. This rule, discovered by Einstein, says you can take the number 72 divided by your interest rate and you'll have the number of years it will take to double your client's money. It's an easy tool to show clients how you can impact their savings.

Let's assume we were selling fixed annuities in the mid-2000s, when CD rates hovered around 4 percent. Using the Rule of 72, we know it would have taken 18 years for your clients to double their money (ignoring taxes and inflation). During the same time, fixed annuities were selling for around 5 percent. That would have allowed you to shorten their money-doubling time to 14.4 years.

In today's rate environment, five-year CDs are paying clients around 1 percent, while a typical fixed annuity is paying around 2.25 percent. You might not think those rates are attractive, but change your attitude by focusing on time, not rates. It would take 72 years for clients to double their money with a 1 percent CD. For clients with a fixed annuity at 2.25 percent, you reduce that cycle down to 32 years. A 40-year difference is far more significant than the four-year difference you would have made in the clients' situation in the mid-2000s.

Re-examine how you think about fixed annuities in the low-rate environment. Focus on the client and how fixed annuities can positively impact their financial position relative to other solutions. When you look at the impact you can deliver, your clients will appreciate the conversation.

Winning Strategy: We need to change how we look at the fixed annuity market. We can have more impact selling a fixed annuity today than we did when an annuity earned 5 percent interest.

Follow your clients, not the herd
February 10, 2014

Too many advisors follow the herd to manage assets without focusing on the client need. This behavior leads us to overlook solutions that clients desire and that will add value to the client/advisor relationship. If we look at products in a different light, we might see new avenues to enhance our clients' portfolios and solve one of their biggest uncertainties – retirement.

Advisors continually tell me that they don't want to lock up their clients' assets with annuities, and advisors tell me their clients don't like all the fees. However, in a 2013 Genworth survey, 91 percent of annuity owners had positive or neutral impressions of them.* When you dig deeper into the survey, you find that 70 percent of annuity owners say the annuity's expenses are worth the benefits they are receiving from it.

Financial professionals need to present annuities to their clients. Nearly 40 percent of the people surveyed who did not own an annuity indicated they would consider buying one but have not been presented the opportunity to do so by their financial professional. This opens a large opportunity to have a meaningful discussion with pre-retirees and prospects about the benefits of re-positioning a portion of their assets into annuities.

Liquidity remains a hurdle for many advisors. It's important to position the correct amount of assets into an annuity when working with clients. However, the same study found 78 percent of people who own annuities are satisfied with the access to their money. More importantly, many new immediate annuities provide liquidity features that allow as much as 90 percent of the period certain to be provided in a lump sum to the annuitant. These features provide ample opportunity for the advisor and client to be flexible in retirement planning.

Winning Strategy: Regardless of your view on annuities, it's time to have a quality conversation with your distributor on the new generation of annuities. You don't know what you don't know until you look at things differently.

"The Future of Retirement Income Study: Putting your clients in control of their future," Genworth, October 9, 2013.

It's All Relative
April 14, 2014

April 3, 1998, was the first time the Dow Jones industrial average reached 9,000 points. Many people thought the index could not go much higher, while others believed in the irrational exuberance of the stock market. Regardless of what you thought at the time, the results since then point to the value of fixed indexed annuities.

At the close of business on April 3, 2014, the Dow closed at 16,572 points. The total rate of return equates to 4.14 percent over a 16-year period. If you consider the impact of capital gains on the investment, the return decreases to 3.52 percent. After assuming a 100bps investment management fee, the real rate of return is 2.52 percent. Fee and tax drag took away nearly 40 percent of the gross return.

Many advisors are telling me that the low cap environment prevents them from showing FIAs to their clients. If you consider that an index would only need to pierce a 4 percent cap 63 percent of the time to beat a 2.52 percent real rate of return, FIAs make a great choice for many clients. Considering there is no market risk associated with FIAs, the client would see a more consistent return than having been in the market over the same period.

Winning Strategy: Relatively speaking, FIAs have performed well over long periods of time against the general market, even in a low interest rate and cap rate environment. Give FIAs a look for the conservative portion of your portfolios. You might find that the FIA portion doesn't create drag in the overall return.

Knowledge is Power
July 3, 2014

In previous posts, I have mentioned the need to understand our clients' behaviors, desires and objectives in order to be a valuable ally in their planning process. It seems advisors aren't always on the same page with consumers, however.

A recent LIMRA study asked consumers and advisors what the top three concerns were in retirement planning.[1] Of course, advisors and consumers agree that running out of money and creating a retirement income plan were very important. Unfortunately, advisors underestimated other components their clients highly prioritized. Clients placed a high value on protecting portfolio principal – they actually valued this 50 percent more than the advisors surveyed. I found this gap alarming as it indicates we might not be addressing our customers' true wishes.

Recently, the Federal Reserve began talking about the "complacency bubble" where clients have become comfortable with risk. In reality, maybe advisors have become comfortable with the recent run in the equity markets, but our clients remain fearful of a major correction. It's worth a conversation with our clients to make sure they remain at the same risk tolerance they are willing to take.

Taking gains off the table may be an appropriate tactic in today's market environment. Fixed indexed annuities provide a tool to sweep gains into qualified accounts while remaining attached to an equity index.

The other large gap the study revealed centered on minimizing taxes. Again, consumers valued this 50 percent more than advisors. With increased tax brackets, higher federal entitlement taxes and alternative minimum tax for high wage earners, the impact of tax deferral has never been more important.

Carriers seem to be focused more on accumulation-driven product design as they try to remove risk from their product portfolios. But for consumers worried about taxes, annuities remain a valuable tool in the planning process. Non-qualified assets gain tax-deferred status during the accumulation phase, while guaranteeing a lifetime income during the payout phase. More importantly, annuities provide tax-efficient distribution during retirement.

Winning Strategy: Annuities can provide lift and calm consumer concerns in many retirement planning strategies. Shielding growth from current taxation allows for quicker accumulation. Leveraging the many distribution options creates a better take-home income stream in many cases. And, the guarantees and safety of annuities can help clients feel secure. Look at how an annuity might fit into your clients' retirement plans.

[1] *"Informing the Debate: Facts About Retirement Security,"* LIMRA, 2014.

Let's Compare Income Values
March 24, 2014

I talk to many advisors who simply sell the guaranteed income rider increases on fixed indexed annuities and variable annuities. That alone creates confusion, as I routinely talk to clients who think they are earning 6 percent or 7 percent on their initial investments. Whether the annuity is being mis-sold or misunderstood remains a topic for another time. What is important is how much leverage the client can create for the assets being deployed for income purposes.

When LIMRA released its 2013 fourth quarter industry statistics, deferred income annuities rose to the fastest growing segment of the annuity market place. It's easy to understand when you look at the alternatives associated with income riders, especially those that bear market risks.

For example, we placed $500,000 in a deferred annuity for a 55-year-old male. The client deferred income for 20 years (to age 75) and began taking a life with installment refund income option. The annuity produced a $9,015 income for life with a refund of unused premium. Assuming a 5 percent payout factor on an income rider at age 75 with a maxed-out income rider, the client would have had to grown an income rider value equal to $1,620,000. I am not aware of an income rider that will generate more than three times the initial premium – guaranteed.

Winning Strategy: It's time to turn the conversation to income, leverage and tax efficiency – not false guarantees of paper value. Our clients need solutions to their biggest fear – outliving their income.

National Annuity Awareness Month
June 1, 2014

National Annuity Awareness Month spotlights the need for a financial vehicle that provides abundant client value and creates predictable income, but comes at the highest level of scrutiny. In June, we need to focus on the real benefits of annuities and maximizing those benefits for our clients.

Tax-deferred growth: With increased tax rates as high as 39.6 percent, it has never been more important to protect the growth of non-qualified savings. At a 3 percent growth factor, a $100,000 account would grow to $134,391 over 10 years. In a taxable account, taxes would account for $14,719. That's $1,400 per year, which will make a significant difference for many Americans.

Alternative income: The average IRA balance at the end of 2012 surged to $81,100, according to a Fidelity Investments analysis of nearly 7 million IRA accounts. For today's near retiree, the reality is that they do not have enough assets to live a comfortable retirement on interest only. We must look at vehicles that provide guaranteed income for basic living expenses. Annuities are the only vehicle that can provide lifetime income and longevity credits to increase payouts.

Peace of mind: More people are afraid of running out of money than they are of public speaking or dying in a plane crash. The year a person runs out of money is not their worst fear, however. It's the months and years leading up to a zero balance that they fear the most. Retirees and their families experience a lot of anxiety knowing their income will diminish and their lifestyle will dramatically change. With a guaranteed stream of income, annuities can provide peace of mind like no other vehicle.

Safety: Annuities continue to be backed by an industry that has not defaulted on its clients. Even through the Great Depression, clients remained whole with the protections of our industry and its state insurance protection. In turbulent times, and uncertainty with interest rates, annuities continue to provide more value to clients than comparable no-risk investments.

Winning Strategy: Many public pundits continue to question the value of annuities, focusing on cost. Instead, our industry needs to turn the conversation to value. We need to focus on delivering solutions to clients needing guaranteed income, safe investments and tax-efficient distributions. Annuities are a great solution for many Americans.

The Cruelest Tax of All

March 31, 2014

"Fundamentals eliminate ways to fail, ways to lose. The greatest fundamentalists – in coaching, warfare, in theology, in business – were and always have been more concerned about losing than winning.
— *Bob Knight, "The Power of Negative Thinking"*

When you talk to some of the most successful coaches in any sport, they focus on eliminating mistakes. At Indiana University, we felt that if we eliminated mistakes (turnovers, giving up offensive rebounds to the other team, giving up easy baskets, or committing too many personal fouls), we gave ourselves a better chance to win any game.

In retirement planning, we tend to focus on rates of return and how to maximize the return. In reality, the successful retirement plan eliminates the potential risks.

Too few times I hear advisors talking to clients about the impact of inflation, for example. Inflation may be the cruelest tax of them all. It is hidden, largely undisclosed until after the fact, and grows exponentially. When clients are concerned about living a long time, inflation is a risk that gets larger every year, and it must be addressed.

Our typical solution is to earn a higher return. In order to do that, you must take greater risks. Unfortunately, you cannot afford to take greater risks with your nest egg as you get closer to distribution or during distribution.

The inflation risk on your client's income can be transferred to an insurance carrier. Annuity distributions can be tied to a number of consumer indices or set to grow at 3-5 percent annually. While they may start at a lower payment initially, it is easier to gain more return early in their retirement years when life expectancy is longer and the time horizon is longer. Over time, these inflation-adjusted income checks increase to well beyond the initial payout structure.

Winning Strategy: Health care costs, food, gas and consumer goods will continue to cost more. Your retirement income needs to produce more in later years. Look at annuities to shift the risk of longevity and inflation away from your clients' portfolios.

Part III

Products

Thoughts from Others

Sweeping Gains Off The Table

By Leighanne Noah - March 5, 2015

Over the last five and half years, we've seen a 192 percent increase in a bull market … it's been a nice ride! However, the average bull market only lasts four years. Are your clients ready for the next big market change?

Even the experts aren't sure how long this performance will last, and our clients are more uncertain than ever about when they will retire. Worker confidence is down 43 percent.[1] With only 19 percent of them having some type of pension outside of Social Security, many are concerned with their accounts taking any losses … and having enough time to make up with gains.

Now, more than ever, clients want the flexibility to turn on income whenever they need … and not be locked in.

Of the 76.4 million baby boomers, the oldest are currently in their 60s, and the youngest are entering their 50s.[2] That puts the median age at 57, and we're finding that 50 percent of retirees are retiring sooner than expected.

So, if a 57-year-old client is still looking to retire at age 65, they have about eight years left. But, in reality, the average retirement age is closer to 62, so they would only have about five years left. Maybe it's time to start looking at age-based, in-service withdrawals. Now might be the time to sweep their gains off the table, locking them in and eliminating risk to their principal.

We've got to ask ourselves: What are the ramifications for staying at the party too long? Do these baby boomers have time to make up for any market losses? What would it take to get back to even? Based off where we are in the market now, where are we going next?

With a fixed indexed annuity, a client near retirement can protect a portion of their portfolio from downturns and still participate in gains. When the market is up, interest is locked in and account value is intact with any growth that might have been credited – not capturing 100 percent of the gain, but protecting the loss to principal when the market goes backwards. Even if the market would be down every year, with a fixed indexed annuity, there still is a minimum guarantee somewhere close to 1 percent.

Winning Strategy: Now is the time to sweep gains off the table and reduce portfolio volatility. Talk to your clients now – you never know when the bull market will end.

[1] "The 2014 Retirement Confidence Survey: Confidence Rebounds – for Those With Retirement Plans," Employee Benefit Research Institute, March 2014.
[2] "The Baby Boom Cohort in the United States: 2012 to 2060," U.S. Census Bureau, May 2014.

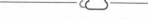

The Right Tool for the Job
By Matt Parke - March 19, 2015

I'm not the handiest person around, so it's no surprise I don't enjoy fixing things around the house. When I do tackle a project, however, the experience is completely different when I have the right tool instead of using something that just gets the job done. The right size socket as opposed to an adjustable wrench, for example.

When it comes to your clients, helping them select the best options on a fixed indexed annuity (FIA) can make it the right tool for retirement income.

We all know that over a longer time horizon you will achieve better returns in the stock market, which makes variable annuities (VAs) with sub-accounts attractive to many clients. During the accumulation phase of building up your portfolio, VAs are an attractive piece of the puzzle. However, coming down the stretch or at the beginning of the withdrawal period, there are several things that work against the variable model and favor a fixed indexed option.

First, we all know that an ill-timed negative year can have a major impact on the value of the account. An FIA takes the negative year off the table. Are you giving up the potential for a larger gain? Yes, but if your client no longer has the time horizon to weather a double-digit negative year, it's a small price to pay. If you're saying, "That's why we have a roll-up and a guaranteed lifetime withdrawal benefit," I agree.

Fees

The fees in the VA are going to be higher than the FIA. The rider fee may be similar, but when you factor in mortality and expense fees, as well as administration and investment fees, your VA could be charging you 3 percent, 3.5 percent or even more. An FIA will limit your fees to somewhere around 1 percent annually.

In distribution, fees become even more critical to your portfolio. If you're taking a 5 percent lifetime distribution and being charged 3 percent per year, are you going to have greater than 8 percent annual returns? If you're using the income rider, does it allow for a portfolio that can generate that type of return, or does it give you limited investment options associated with the rider? I think you would have to agree that your VA is no longer an accumulation vehicle.

Sequence of Returns

Just as important as the fees is the sequence of returns. If you're arguing that you are using the VA to maintain an account value or grow the asset during distribution, a double-digit negative year can make that prospect almost impossible. Obviously, a repeat of 2008 would be devastating to any allocation, but even during the early years of distribution, a 15 percent decrease would be difficult to overcome. Add in the fees, and what would it take to see an increase in income or maintain your account value?

Fixed Indexed Advantages

Now that we are looking for an annuity that works as a distribution tool, why is an FIA a better option? FIAs offer your clients:

- Higher roll-up rates than you will find in VAs, which allow for greater guaranteed income potential
- Higher distribution rates, which allow for higher guaranteed payments in retirement
- Increasing payout options that aren't tied to the account value, eclipsing the income value
- Fees only associated with the benefit of having a guaranteed income that you cannot outlive
- No negative performance impacts to the account

Winning Strategy: An FIA can be the right tool for the income portion of your client's annuity portfolio. The right product and rider can be an efficient income generator to meet their income needs for a lifetime.

Don't Forget this Solution for Businesses
By Steve Pilger - January 15, 2015

We all know annuities are a great solution for retirement. But, have you ever considered annuities as a retirement solution for businesses? If you're working with business owners and executive-level clients, ask if their company has a defined benefit pension plan.

Why? Traditional pension plans have become a thing of the past as 401(k) and other contributory plans have overtaken the retirement landscape. As a result, many businesses have decided to do two things:

1. Freeze and eventually terminate an existing defined benefit pension plan

2. Shift all or a portion of their plan benefit obligations to a third party

Here's how it works: Businesses with a defined benefit pension plan can remove plan liabilities from their books by transferring the risk to a group annuity issued by a top-rated insurance company. This transfer allows the company to eliminate premiums paid to the Pension

Benefit Guaranty Corporation along with significant cost savings in the plan administration.

These cost savings can be reinvested in their business. Most importantly, the transfer allows the company to make good on the benefit promises made to their employees.

Plan participants benefit from the transfer because it ensures payment of the plan benefits promised to them at retirement, which may include guaranteed income, the ability to provide ongoing income for a joint annuitant, and options such as payment frequency or cost-of-living adjustments.

Winning Strategy: Annuities aren't just for individuals. Ask your business owners if they feel secure with their defined benefit pension plans.

Help Minimize the Impact of RMDs

By Jason Richardson - March 12, 2015

Who would've ever guessed that one day we'd be saying, "I may actually live longer than expected"? It's true – we're actually living longer! According to data compiled by the Social Security Administration:

- A man reaching age 65 today can expect to live, on average, until age 84.3
- A woman turning age 65 today can expect to live, on average, until age 86.6*

Those are just averages – the SSA also reports about one out of every four 65-year-olds today will live past age 90, and one out of 10 will live past age 95.

Since we can expect to live longer, then we need to help our clients' retirement funds live longer as well. QLACs (Qualified Longevity Annuity Contracts) are one new option to help ensure your clients don't outlive their income. These long-term investments designed for retirement income planning are a contract between your client and an insurance company. Though annuities are not new, QLACs were only introduced to the market last year.

On July 1, 2014, the U.S. Department of Treasury and IRS issued the final rules regarding deferred income annuities (DIAs), thereby deeming longevity annuities that meet specific requirements QLACs. Like all annuities, QLACs help retirees plan for their retirement by using a portion of their savings to purchase a guaranteed income stream. This income stream is backed by the financial strength and claims-paying ability of the issuing insurance company. With QLACs, however, this income stream begins much later in life.

By purchasing a QLAC, retirees can reduce their RMDs (required minimum distributions) by up to 25 percent (a maximum of $125,000) and not have to take distribution on those funds until later (up through age 85). This is not ideal for all clients, but it's a good opportunity for clients who aren't using their RMDs for necessary income.

Carriers had to create specialty DIAs to meet QLAC guidelines. They started rolling out products at the end of 2014 - more are likely coming soon.

Winning Strategy: As your clients approach retirement and their life expectancies increase, QLACs can help them hedge the risk of outliving their retirement income.

"SSA Calculators: Life Expectancy," March 1, 2015.

Buy High and Reset Low!

By Steve Schankerman - January 26, 2015

In a traditional investment, the goal is to buy low and sell high. However, most investors end up buying high and selling low. With the stock market at an all-time high, you should have a conversation with your clients about a fixed indexed annuity.

When talking about a fixed indexed annuity, please remember:

- Money in a fixed indexed annuity will not suffer from a market decline (principal protection)
- If there is a market decline, the client will receive a zero percent rate of return for that year, and the starting point for

the upcoming anniversary year will be at the new lower point

- Taxes on growth are deferred
- The client has penalty-free access to a portion of the account value each year
- Annuities offer the opportunity to create a guaranteed income for life

Winning Strategy: Fixed indexed annuities can be a great option for clients who want to get better yields without risk to principal. Consider buying while the market's high.

Crediting methods: Options for filling your clients' buckets

By Steve Schankerman - December 18, 2014

A lot of advisors think of crediting methods like buckets. Most fixed indexed annuities use a one-year crediting method, so your client gets whatever is in the bucket at the end of the year. The bucket is dumped out annually (reset) and everything starts over.

If you have a three-year crediting method, the bucket isn't emptied until the third year. So, if the market has a weak first year (little in the bucket or leaks), but it recovers in the second and third (takes on lots of water), your client could come out ahead. They would have a lot more water in the bucket at the end of the third year than at the end of the first.

However, let's say the opposite happens – the market has a good first year (lots of water) but stumbles in the second and third (a few leaks in the bucket). Your client could lose out on those returns from the first year and get less than they would have with the one-year option.

Despite the potential for smaller returns, the multi-year crediting option offers several advantages. The pricing on these annuities is usually lower, with higher caps, lower spreads and higher participation rates.

Remember, it's possible to have a negative return with any crediting method, and we can't predict market performance. Some clients and advisors simply can't wait three whole years to see their results – others wouldn't mind waiting for more.

Winning Strategy: If you have a client who's a little more patient and wants more upside potential, look at longer crediting options. It may take time, but their bucket could be filled to the brim.

Rollovers Now Restricted

By Mike Senkier - January 19, 2015

Be aware: An IRS clarification that took effect Jan. 1, 2015, now restricts IRA rollovers. Your clients can make only one rollover from any of their IRAs to another (or the same) IRA in a 12-month period, regardless of the type or number of IRAs they own.

This one-per-year limit applies across all IRAs in the aggregate including traditional, Roth, SIMPLE and SEP IRAs.

Before Jan. 1, the one-per-year limit applied on an IRA-by-IRA basis. This change in the IRS's interpretation of the one-per-year rule comes from the U.S. Tax Court's decision in Bobrow v. Commissioner.

If your clients make more than one rollover in a 12-month period, the improper rollovers may be subject to the following tax consequences:

- Any previously untaxed amounts may be taxable
- If they were under age 59 ½ when they took the distribution, they may be subject to an additional 10 percent early withdrawal tax
- All or a portion of the improper rollover may be treated as an excess contribution and be subject to an additional penalty tax of 6 percent per year for each year that the excess contribution remains in the IRA

Your clients can still continue to do as many of the following transactions in a 12 month-period as they want:

- Trustee-to-trustee transfers between IRAs
- Rollovers from traditional IRAs to Roth IRAs (i.e., "conversions")

- Rollovers between qualified plans and IRAs

Winning Strategy: Make sure you understand the new IRS rules before you make any client recommendations this year.

RMD, QLAC, IRA, DIA – What does it all mean? Action!

By Jason Caudill - October 27, 2014

If your practice is anything like mine, activity is a critical component in driving revenue-generating opportunities. The IRS and U.S. Treasury put new required minimum distribution (RMD) regulations into place effective July 1, 2014, and in doing so, gave us an opportunity to increase activity that will drive sales in the fourth quarter of 2014 and into 2015.

These new regulations implement suggestions made in 2010, in response to the Obama administration's request for information on lifetime income options. The new regulations allow an individual retirement account (IRA) owner to use a portion of their qualified money to purchase a qualified longevity annuity contract (QLAC) and have that portion exempt from RMD calculations.

A QLAC in our language is a deferred immediate annuity (DIA). It's very important to note that a QLAC must be a DIA fixed contract issued from a carrier – no private annuities are allowed. Additionally, fixed indexed annuities and variable annuities don't meet the regulations.

Now you have a great reason to contact clients who aren't using their RMDs and show them a way to continue to defer taxes on a portion of their qualified assets. These recent changes to IRS rules have many benefits:

- Your clients may defer 25 percent of their qualified assets, up to a maximum of $125,000
- DIAs are the least expensive way to purchase a guaranteed future income stream, and purchasing today allows your clients to take advantage of today's mortality credits. For example: a 70-year-old male purchasing a $100,000 DIA from an A++ carrier today could guarantee themselves a $30,698.76 annual

income beginning at age 85 (life with cash refund)

- Income can be deferred up to age 85, and as a result, taxes are too
- A number of death benefit options are now eligible, including return of premium

While DIAs are available today, the first QLAC-friendly contract is expected to be released at the beginning of November, with more expected to follow. According to LIMRA, DIAs were the fastest growing annuity segment in 2013, and they are expected to capture significantly more market share in the years ahead.

Winning Strategy: Now is a great time to reach out to your clients who don't enjoy taking RMDs – schedule a meeting to discuss this new opportunity. Activity will lead to sales, even if it doesn't involve utilizing this concept.

Are You Limiting Your Clients' Potential?
By Paul Gauger - March 26, 2015

At the moment, the average seven-year fixed annuity is yielding right around 2.5 percent. To CD consumers, this rate sounds surprisingly appealing. In my experience, I feel that far too many advisors and their clients set their eyes on a fixed, multi-year guarantee annuity as being the one and only alternative to CDs and/or other investment vehicles for money they want to keep protected. Fixed indexed annuities are overlooked, even though they provide the exact same principal protection while offering the potential for gains in the neighborhood of 5 percent.

Let's look at some facts ...

- In the last 30 years, the S&P 500 has had positive growth 24 times
- Out of those 24 years, growth has been 5 percent or more 18 times
- Conclusion: The S&P 500 has seen growth of 5 percent or more 18 out of the last 30 years (60 percent) – this is an

important statistic, so please keep it in mind

A conservative consumer may feel comfortable earning a 2.5 percent fixed rate on their money for seven years. However, the facts above support an indexed annuity's propensity to outperform a traditional fixed annuity over time.

Here's why: Assuming a premium of $100,000, a traditional seven-year fixed annuity with an annual yield of 2.50 percent will result in an ending value of $118,869. No more, no less. Currently, our best seven-year fixed indexed annuity annual point-to-point cap (S&P 500) for a $100,000 premium is 5 percent. According to the facts stated earlier, the S&P 500 has seen growth of 5 percent or more 18 out of the last 30 years, which is 60 percent.

So, if the seven-year indexed annuity lives up to expectations and performs at this 60 percent average, we'd be looking at hitting the 5 percent cap four out of seven years. This would equate to an ending value of $121,551 – earning the client an additional $2,600 more than the fixed annuity.

Of course, we can't guarantee the indexed annuity's performance, but one argument for an indexed annuity over a fixed annuity is potential. If we hit the annual cap five out of seven years, this will result in an additional $8,700 more than the fixed annuity. Hitting the cap seven out of seven years will give them an additional $21,800.

Winning Strategy: I challenge you to take the time to analyze the facts and benefits behind a fixed indexed annuity. If you aren't talking about them with your clients, someone else will.

The Cost of Waiting
By Brad Harruff - January 8, 2015

We've been in a declining interest rate environment for about the last 10 years, with historically low rates the last few years. These low rates are driven by the Federal Reserve in hopes of jumpstarting the economy by allowing consumers to borrow money cheaply. While lower rates may sound good, they also mean very low returns for products such as

CDs and money market accounts.

Even in this low-interest-rate environment, it's estimated there's still nearly $10 trillion on the sidelines in the form of CDs and money market accounts. Many of these investors are concerned that committing their money to an annuity at current rates won't allow them to take advantage of higher rates in the future. What they may not be considering is that waiting could cause them to lose earnings that may require years to make up, even if they do get a higher rate of return in the future.

For example, if you put $100,000 into an annuity paying 2.25 percent for five years, you would be guaranteed $111,768. If you waited two years before buying that annuity and were earning 0.50 percent in a CD, you would have to earn 3.78 percent over three years in order to get to the same $111,768 you would have been guaranteed with the five-year annuity.

Regardless of interest rates, annuities are really designed for investors' long-term goals. Annuities offer tax deferral, principal protection, liquidity, lifetime income options and death benefits that are paid directly to the beneficiaries.

Winning Strategy: With $10 trillion on the sidelines, now's a great time to reach out to investors about the benefits of tax-deferred annuities.

Start the Long-Term Care Conversation
By Bentley Heese - March 2, 2015

We often use annuities to protect our clients from longevity – the risk of outliving their income. But annuities can also help protect against another risk of living longer – the risk of needing long-term care.

Statistics show that almost 70 percent of the population will need long-term care[1], but less than 8 percent of people have traditional long-term care insurance.[2]

Many advisors do not discuss the topic with their clients and view the LTC conversation as arduous; clients seem to be laissez faire or in denial that they will need some sort of care. Those with assets often state that they will use up some "safe" money (like a CD or money market) in their time of need. However, it's not uncommon to deplete those resources at a rate of $5,000 to $10,000 per month for various types of home care or nursing home services.[3]

Consider the leverage of a linked benefit annuity. With today's evolving world of solutions, there are annuities that combine a powerful leverage and tax advantaged treatment of care coverage – think Pension Protection Act if funds are nonqualified. The client spends down their contract value and, if still on claim, the leverage factor begins after that. The fee is deducted from some contracts; others are more modular but the cost is generally less than traditional LTC plans.

Do you have any clients with old, nonqualified annuity contracts that are out of surrender with a low cost basis and a minimum guaranteed rate better than currently available? Do you have any clients who have asked about traditional LTC but have backed away because they could not grasp the value? Start having conversations with these clients, asking them what they would liquidate first if they experienced a health event and are unable to do two of the six activities of daily living.

These plans are not for the uninsurable, but the process isn't as rigorous as traditional, standalone LTC insurance and generally consists of a questionnaire, phone interview and medical information. If your client never has a need, the contract value is the death benefit. There are many options depending on the source of funds and the leverage your client is looking for.

Winning Strategy: Consider linked benefit options to protect your clients not only from the risk of outliving their income, but also from the potential costs of LTC.

[1] *"The Basics: Who Needs Care?" LongTermCare.gov, U.S. Department of Health and Human Services.*
[2] *"Long-Term Care: What Are the Issues?" Robert Wood Johnson Foundation, February 2014.*
[3] *"Costs & How to Pay: Costs of Care," LongTermCare.gov, U.S. Department of Health and Human Services.*

It's Coming: Protecting Assets from a Market Correction

By Jeff Hood - February 19, 2015

In the game of investments, how many times have we heard the old adage, "Buy low and sell high"? In a perfect world, that's what all investors do. In reality, the opposite happens – more frequently than we'd like to admit.

The game of investments isn't really a game because all players are at risk of losing – losing assets they need for income, retirement, savings, etc. An imminent market correction increases that risk. We've enjoyed the market's highs, but we know it will likely see some real lows. When is the next correction coming? Tomorrow, next week, next month? History tells us it will be soon, though we can't predict exactly when.

So how can players protect their assets from a market correction? Annuities are one option. A fixed annuity guarantees a fixed rate of return over a time period you choose. As a general rule, the rate of return increases with the length of the time period.

Some investors want more than just guaranteed returns, however. They don't want to miss out on market gains. A fixed indexed annuity allows both. Its rate of return is tied to gains in a specific index, such as the S&P 500, and its principal is protected from market losses.

Winning Strategy: Both of these annuities are guaranteed to protect assets when the next correction comes. Talk to your clients about their options before they lose anything in the game of investments.

History and a Math Lesson

By Randy Kitzmiller - January 5, 2015

Why do we study history? Because it's all we have, and history tends to repeat itself. Well, what have we learned from the Japanese economic collapse of the early '90s? Apparently, not much.

Since their real estate bubble burst, Japan has been in a low-interest-rate environment for the last 20 years, yet we keep waiting for interest rates to go up. Right now, billions of dollars are sitting in low-yield fixed accounts earning less than 1 percent, waiting for a rate increase.

We've now been waiting approximately five years for this "rising rate" phenomenon – when will we stop waiting and move on?

So there's your history lesson. Now, let me explain the math lesson. Do you know how significant it can be to find just one percent more yield on your clients' conservative assets today versus five years ago?

Five years ago, a five-year CD was yielding approximately 5 percent interest. If I could have found something to get that client 1 percent more yield, I would have increased their yield by 25 percent. As we stand today, a five-year national CD yield is averaging about 1percent. If I could find something to get that client 1 percent more yield, I could increase their yield by 100 percent!

You could certainly do that, simply by repositioning your clients' assets in a fixed indexed annuity. With cap rates in the 3-4 percent range, it's likely you will find your clients 1 percent more yield without risk to their principal.

So the next time your children ask you, "Why do we study history and math?" you now have your answer.

Winning Strategy: Don't talk yourself out of presenting annuities to your clients because YOU don't believe they will be interested. Clients are seeking yields without risk to principal, and they are finally fed up with sub-1 percent yields.

The Tortoise and the Hare, Revisited
By Randy Kitzmiller - February 12, 2015

As kids, we all learned the story of the tortoise and the hare. As a matter of fact, I ran across an old Bugs Bunny cartoon last week, and it took me back to my childhood. Anyway, the hare reminded me that this story can be used in today's economic environment.

If you can eliminate the downside of any portfolio, you don't need to have nearly the upside possibility to keep up. Let me explain.

You have an equity portfolio of $100,000, and the market is up 12 percent in the first year. What's your balance? One hundred percent of people answer correctly: $112,000.

But if the market is down 12 percent in the next year, most people will answer that they still have $100,000 left, because the average return mathematically is zero. The answer is actually $98,560 – you've lost 12 percent of the $112,000, which is $13,440.

Now, throw a fixed index annuity into the mix with a 5 percent cap rate. On the surface, it's not terribly exciting, like the tortoise. But the beauty is that in the first year you lock in the 5 percent gain, and your balance, even with the down 12 percent year, is $105,000. It beats the equity portfolio by $6,440.

I'm not here to tell you that an FIA will beat a market return in the long-term. What I am saying is that a percentage of every client's portfolio should have the protection of an FIA to smooth out market fluctuations.

Winning Strategy: If you can eliminate the risk of losing money with a portion of your clients' assets in an FIA, you don't need the full upside of the market to keep pace.

Retirement in a Post-'82 NQ World

By Randy Kitzmiller - January 22, 2015

For those of you who've been in the business quite some time, the date Aug. 13, 1982, is hardwired into your memory. For those of you who haven't, it was the day the taxation of nonqualified (NQ) deferred annuities changed from FIFO (first in, first out) to LIFO (last in, first out).

The planning point of a pre-'82 NQ annuity was that you could recover your basis first before any taxable event occurred. For post-'82 annuities, it's interest out first, until you get to basis, then it's return of basis.

Believe it or not, this strategy still exists with NQ monies, with a few caveats. In a world where income planning and taxation is paramount, this strategy may be huge for an income planning case.

Here is how this concept works. Say a client, age 55, with a spouse also age 55, has $100,000 of NQ money to invest. They plan on retiring at age 65, so they have 10 years until income is needed from this deposit. They would place this in a fixed, deferred annuity with an indexed minimum guaranteed withdrawal benefit. The annuity isn't designed for accumulation, only income. Therefore, in the 10th year, should they decide to walk away, the value would still only be $100,000.

But therein is the positive of this concept. In year 11, the guaranteed income for life is $7,988 over two lives. This is about the equivalent of a 6 percent compounded rollup with a 4.5 percent payout rate. Here's the home run: Since it's a deferred annuity with a guaranteed minimum withdrawal benefit, the withdrawals are FIFO since there's no additional cash value in the contract. Therefore, the first 10 years of income are return-of-premium and tax-free.

Once the principal is recovered, it's all taxable. But think of the planning possibilities here! If you could have your first five to 10 years of retirement income-tax-free, think of the possibility of converting some of your qualified monies to Roth IRA, as well as the possibility of delaying Social Security to age 70 to maximize benefits.

Throw in the fact you can now move up to 25 percent of your IRA money to a Qualified Longevity Annuity Contract and avoid required minimum distributions to age 85, and now you have some pretty creative income planning scenarios to work with – not just putting monies into an annuity with an income rider and turning it on at 65!

Winning Strategy: A lot changed in 1982, and a lot has changed since then. Talk to your clients about strategies to maximize their income and minimize their taxes in retirement.

Increasing Client Cash Flow with Temporary Life

By Jim Martin - February 26, 2015

On entering the insurance business, I learned I should do two things: Uncover the need and find the money to pay for that need. A prospect with a need – but not the means to pay for it – isn't really a prospect. Obviously, the more money you can find, the more of the need that can be met.

Frequently, you can fulfill a need and find the money by suggesting your prospect purchase a single-premium immediate annuity (SPIA) and using the annual payments for life insurance premiums. This creates a systematic process for the client and provides the funds just when they are needed to pay the premium. Additionally, it provides you with two sales opportunities.

Many times, in wealth transfer situations for older clients, a limited-pay option may be utilized, e.g., 10-pay life paired with a 10-pay certain SPIA. Hypothetically, let's assume a $100,000 SPIA paid out 10 payments of $10,000. What if that same $100,000 instead generated 10 payments of $11,000? Wouldn't your client now be able to afford more insurance? Alternately, if the SPIA payout is increased, your client may be able to generate the same $10,000 premium for less than $100,000, say $92,000.

The temporary life payout option gives your client greater purchasing power and cash flow. The key difference between a 10-year temporary life payout and a 10-year certain payout, which may normally be used, is that the temporary life option pays out for the lesser of 10 years or death. Because a chance exists that the payouts might stop prior to the 10-year guaranteed period, the amount of the payments increases. The older the client, the greater the chance of death prior to the 10-year period, so the greater the payout differential. For older clients, payout differentials in the double digits are not uncommon.

Winning Strategy: Utilizing the Temporary Life payout option may result in increased cash flow, enabling your clients to fill more of their critical need for insurance protection and providing greater revenue to your practice.

The Forest for the Trees

By Jim Martin - February 9, 2015

Within the fixed indexed annuity (FIA) marketplace, volatility controlled (VC) index options are the talk of the town. Developed to increase the attractiveness of FIA returns in a low-interest-rate environment, these new crediting strategies present something new and interesting to consider.

However, without a full understanding of the underlying mechanics and, more importantly, the setting of realistic expectation of their potential returns, these new indexes could turn into a new reason for a client to be confused and turned off.

It's easy to lose sight of the forest for the trees when discussing these indexes. It's critical to remember the attractiveness of an FIA rests in its simplicity, insulation from market losses, periodic lock in of gains, and its ability to provide lifetime income, even increasing income, all for no to low annual fees. No individual index should overshadow or distract from this package of benefits.

VC crediting strategies were designed to potentially increase the overall return on FIAs. A VC option should be used if a client is looking to increase their accumulation value, increase or extend their residual death benefit, or increase their lifetime income by either outperforming a rollup or providing more punch to an increasing income option.

VC indexes vary significantly in structure and design. Some use spreads, while others use participation rates and/or longer crediting terms. Many are uncapped. It's important to understand the underlying indexes and to be comfortable with their transparency. You should also understand how the indexes are managed and will respond under various market conditions.

Winning Strategy: Make sure you understand the latest hot topics and how they could impact your clients before you start making recommendations.

—————————— ⟨◯⟩ ——————————

Positioning an Indexed Annuity vs. a CD

By Jason Caudill - April 16, 2014

By now I think it's safe to say we're all aware CD rates continue to sit at all-time lows. According to bankrate.com today, the average five-year CD has an interest rate of 0.79 percent.

For retirees who are using the interest from a CD as income, this is very unfortunate. Through no fault of their own, their income is being reduced by as much as 75 percent as these CDs mature.

Due to this low-rate environment, many CD buyers are looking for options and are now willing to consider an annuity when they may not have in the past.

- Example: Seven-year indexed annuity with an investment of $100,000
- Fixed-rate strategy: 2 percent (locked in for seven years on monies initially deposited)
- Performance Trigger: 4.15 percent

Clients who are considering renewing their five-year CD at 1 percent would generate $1,000 of interest annually. However, with this same $100,000, they could place $50,000 into a fixed-rate strategy to generate the same $1,000 of interest, then position the remaining $50,000 into the performance-trigger account at 4.15 percent. If the S&P 500 ends negative, the client will still earn the same $1,000 from the fixed strategy. However, if the S&P is flat or positive, they earn an extra $2,075 for the year.

Winning Strategy: An indexed annuity could be a great way to generate a significantly better return for these investors while guaranteeing protection of their principal investment.

No Better Time for Advisors

By John Duchien - May 2, 2014

When you look back on your career in financial services, has there ever been a better time to be a financial advisor? Has there ever been a time when sound financial planning has been more needed than right now? Clients have access to more information, more analyses and more financial opinions than ever before. The result? More confusion. More fear. More doubt as to which direction to take.

Just turn on your favorite financial network, and listen to the well-credentialed featured guest telling you exactly what to expect from the financial markets in the days ahead. The arguments are well thought out and convincing. But, after the next commercial break, a new guest is introduced ... Equally credentialed. Equally compelling. The only problem is that this guest is making the exact opposite predictions for the future of the financial markets. Is there any wonder why clients are so confused and in need of your services more than ever?

When you recommend fixed and indexed annuities, your clients will appreciate having the opportunity to earn reasonable rates of return without having to worry about the preservation of their principal. Additionally, when appropriate, you also can enhance the annuity value by adding a death benefit, a lifetime income rider or a long-term care rider. In doing so, your clients can feel comfortable with the direction of their financial future.

Winning Strategy: There truly has never been a better time to be a financial advisor. Help your clients find clarity rather than confusion, and you'll find success.

Two-Thirds Right

By John Duchien - November 10, 2014

When financial markets become more volatile, as they have over the past few months, clients tend to seek safety. After all, increasing volatility was the first indicator of the tech bubble from 2000 to 2003 and the financial crisis in 2008. It's no wonder conservative clients are anxious to avoid another potentially significant retreat in the stock market.

Clients are afraid of doing the wrong thing at the wrong time – that's why there are trillions of dollars still sitting on the sidelines. As their financial advisor, you can assuage those fears by positioning index annuities as a significant percentage of their portfolio. With the two-thirds strategy, they can take advantage of any market conditions.

Here's how it works:

1. Your clients position one-third of their assets in mutual funds, variable annuities or other managed equity investments

2. They position one-third of their assets into fixed annuities and one-third into indexed annuities

Once this positioning is complete, your clients have two-thirds of their assets positioned to take advantage of any market eventuality.

If the stock market turns negative, the one-third in fixed annuities would be earning the stated interest rate, while the indexed annuity would at worst be unchanged by the sinking market. In fact, if the index annuity has an annual reset crediting method, the starting point for the subsequent year would be lower, making it more likely for a positive return.

If the stock market stays positive and continues to set all-time highs, your clients will still have two-thirds positioned to take advantage. The one-third in mutual funds or variable annuities will grow along with the market, and the one-third positioned in the indexed annuities will also be earning competitive returns based on the crediting method.

With this strategy, your clients can feel comfortable that they will always have two-thirds of their assets positioned to take advantage of market conditions. For more conservative clients, you might want to use the same concept, but raise the level to three-quarters or even four-fifths.

Three-quarters:
- 25 percent fixed annuities
- 50 percent indexed annuities
- 25 percent mutual funds/variable annuities

Four-fifths:
- 20 percent fixed annuities
- 60 percent indexed annuities
- 20 percent mutual funds/variable annuities

Winning Strategy: You can change the allocation based on the ages and risk tolerances of your clients. If nothing else, the discussion of the above strategies will open up a dialog of the features and benefits of fixed and indexed annuities, as well as other equity investments.

The Great Debate: CDs vs. Annuities

By Brad Harruff - December 4, 2014

When looking for safe investment options, many investors look to CDs, especially when equity investments are on the downturn. Many seem to think CDs are the only option that can provide safety and guaranteed growth. However, tax-deferred annuities compare very favorably to CDs, and investors should review both products' features to help determine which is best suited for their financial situation:

Tax Savings – Annuity gains grow tax-deferred, while interest earned on CDs is taxed and reported annually as ordinary income. Taking advantage of tax deferral will increase your earning power by continued annual earnings on your tax savings.

Earnings on annuities are taxed as ordinary income when withdrawals are made. However, you do have an option to spread out the tax burden for nonqualified money through guaranteed income payments, where payments are partly returned on non-taxed cost basis.

Earning Power – As of October 2014, the average return on a one-year CD was 0.26 percent, and the average for a five-year CD was 0.83 percent. At the same time, the average five-year fixed annuity rate was 1.63 percent – a tax equivalent yield of 2.26 percent, based on a 28 percent tax bracket.

Investors could also take advantage of tax-deferred indexed annuities to provide even more earning potential. These products include many indexing options, including un-capped strategies, with no downside risk to principal.

Lifetime Income Options – Tax-deferred annuities offer guaranteed lifetime income payments through annuitization or lifetime income riders. These are great retirement planning tools that generate income you can't outlive. CDs can be liquidated as they mature, but there's no guarantee the funds will last a lifetime.

Liquidity – Annuities allow up to 10 percent of the value to be withdrawn without penalty. With CDs, withdrawals prior to maturity are generally subject to penalties.

Payment at Death – Annuities can help avoid probate by paying funds directly to the beneficiary. CDs, however, are subject to probate, along with possible costs and delays.

Winning Strategy: CDs aren't the only safe investment option available. Make sure your clients see how the features of an annuity compare and can potentially offer them more benefits.

Fear and Greed and Annuities

By Bentley Heese - May 22, 2014

Way back in the dark ages (pre-Internet), nearly 30 years ago, I earned my bachelor's degree in psychology. Throughout my sales career, it has been enlightening and affirming to observe just how much of what we feel, believe and perceive is governed by our emotions.

The investor experience is wrought with visceral emotion, much to the chagrin of those who do not seek any professional guidance. Human nature compels us to buy high and sell low.

When I studied for my licenses, I took batteries of tests, studying many terms and investment scenarios. Nowhere was there any mention of controlling investor emotions and expectations. As an advisor, you have to control two powerful client emotions: fear and greed. The overall strong 2013 stock market is a recent example, as some clients are now expecting higher returns and overall portfolio performance.

Now, more than ever, it is important that you manage your clients' expectations, along with their fear and greed. Fixed Indexed Annuities (also known as Equity Indexed Annuities) may be a great part of your clients' portfolios, and they may address all three of these challenges.

FIAs remove fear from the equation with their downside protection. Zero is your hero when an index is way down on the anniversary date. The annual re-set creates a new starting point and upside opportunity for your client for the following year. When an index is up, you have satisfied their greed as long as you have set the proper expectations regarding the upside potential. Don't make it complicated or confuse your client; remember an FIA is simply a fixed annuity with a different way to credit interest.

Winning Strategy: Today's FIA solutions have evolved tremendously from just a few years ago. Whether your clients' require income, seek accumulation or are looking for bond alternatives and safe money vehicles, be ready to help them satisfy their emotions.

Do Not Talk Yourself Out of Annuity Sales

By Randy Kitzmiller - October 20, 2014

I would challenge every advisor in this business to ask yourself the following question: Are YOU talking yourself out of fixed or fixed indexed annuity sales because YOU think they're not a good value for your customers?

In my travels, I often come across new advisors who cannot believe that fixed and fixed indexed annuity sales are having a record year. They actually seem to feel sorry for me until I explain now is a great time to be in the business.

Right now, clients are looking for ways to get better yields without risk. There has NEVER been a better time to sell these products since other low-risk alternatives are at all-time lows for returns. I always compare the value of an annuity against a five-year CD. Back in 2008, you could find a fixed annuity rate at 5 percent, with indexed annuity caps around 8 percent. Five-year CDs were also at about 5 percent. So the leverage between the CD and the fixed annuity was nothing, and the index cap came out a little ahead.

Today's rates are a different story. Five-year CDs are at 1 percent, with a five-year fixed annuity at about 2 percent and index caps about 5 percent. The leverage for the fixed annuity is now two times the CD, and the index cap five times! So I would argue that now's a much better time to sell these products than five years ago, not to mention we also now have very innovative income riders available.

Winning Strategy: Don't talk yourself out of annuity sales – the public is starving for them!

Numbers are Telling a New Story

By Dan Lavigne - September 11, 2014

Our industry story used to read something like this: Markets are up and so are variable annuity sales, or rates are up and so are fixed annuity sales. Today, it's the opposite: The market is up while variable sales are down, and rates are down while fixed annuity sales are up.

The numbers don't lie. A recent LIMRA Secure Retirement Institute report showed total fixed annuity sales up 34 percent from last year, while variable annuity sales fell 5 percent. Fixed indexed annuities set a new quarterly record of $13 billion, up 40 percent over sales last year, capturing 52 percent of the total fixed annuity sales for the first time ever.[1]

It appears this is a new twist on our old story. So, when I first saw this data, I asked many questions:

- With rates so low and the market on the rise for nearly five straight years, who would possibly be interested in a fixed annuity?
- Why aren't variable annuity sales through the roof?
- Do the sales of the advisors I work with fall in line with these numbers?
- Is this the start of a real trend? Or is this just another fad in the financial services industry?

Let's review a couple of basic truths to see if we can reveal some answers.

- The aging population still doesn't feel safe in the market
- Even after a prolonged attempt by the Fed to force investors into riskier assets, there's still nearly $10 trillion on the sidelines in the form of CDs and money market accounts
- Added to the $3.5 trillion in short-term bond funds, we have nearly the same amount of money in safe asset classes (earning less than 1 percent per year) as we have in 401(k)s and IRAs combined

In talking to the advisors I work closely with, I've come to realize that their numbers do in fact fall in line with the LIMRA numbers, and many of them are having their best years ever. They've embraced the concept that some people are investors while others are savers. Savers will never become investors, no matter how hard the Fed pushes, and they're starved for safe alternatives. Advisors who are truly listening to the desires of the savers say they're having a real impact on their business and their clients.

Winning Strategy: Most fads fade out after five to 10 years, and this movement just seems to be getting started. In fact, it looks like it could go parabolic over the next decade, especially as many of our investors look to become maintainers. So I guess the real question is: If you're not making fixed and fixed indexed annuity sales to your clients, then who is?

---

[1]*"LIMRA Secure Retirement Institute: Total Annuity Sales Improve Eight Percent in Second Quarter 2014," LIMRA, August 18, 2014.*

———————— ⌓ ————————

Make It or Take It?

By Jim Martin - May 7, 2014

Whether your prospects are more concerned with "Making It" (accumulation) or "Taking It" (locking in the highest amount of retirement income) or both, recent innovations in fixed indexed annuities (FIAs) can meet their needs.

Perhaps it sounds too similar to the inflammatory and divisive stereotype of the American public during a presidential election, but identifying where your prospects stand on the "Make It — Take It" scale can prove invaluable in leveraging recent product enhancements for FIA products.

Make It

FIAs have been criticized recently for having caps that are "too low," thus limiting earning potential. While caps are historically on the lower end, significant opportunity still exists.

Uncapped Option – Designed to minimize the effect of volatility in today's markets, this dynamically managed option shows well historically and may provide the growth potential your prospects are looking for or need, to make up lost ground. (100 percent participation rate with annual spread)

Uncapped option + 50 percent – Add a reasonable policy fee or wait to take income for 10 years (still well below those on VAs) and your prospect will receive an additional boost to their annual index returns.

Take It

Increasing Payout Percentage – Not your standard age-banded payout percentage, this rider provides an annually increasing payout percentage for each year the contract is in accumulation.

A 50-year-old client, after a 10 years of accumulation, can lock in a 5.5 percent to 7.0 percent payout. (Selection based on single/joint, level/increasing payout at time income is taken – not at issue!) With a 20-year hold, the range increases from 8.5 percent to 10 percent.

A 60-year-old client, after a 10 years of accumulation, can lock in a 7.5 percent to 9.0 percent payout. (Again, selection based on single/ joint, level/increasing payout at time income is taken—not at issue!) With a 20-year hold, the range increases to 9.0 percent to 13 percent.

Many consumers are purchasing this rider primarily to lock in these percentage options.

Increasing Lifetime Income at Payout – If income is important now, won't it be even more so in the future? Regardless of the severity of future inflation, prospects must plan for the need for even more income in the future.

This feature enables your prospect's future guaranteed lifetime income to increase every time there is an index credit earned – even if the account value goes to $0. While this doesn't mean guaranteed annual income increases, it does provide for welcomed income increases periodically.

Winning Strategy: Allocating a portion of you prospect's portfolio to a FIA with a combination of uncapped growth, uncapped growth with guaranteed increasing payout percentages, and/or guaranteed lifetime increasing income can provide your prospects with a cost-effective means to increase their comfort in retirement, be they "Makers or Takers."

The Best 'Worst Case' Alternative

By Jim Martin - August 14, 2014

"The best 'worst case' alternative" – that's how a large variable annuity producer recently described and positioned fixed indexed annuities with income riders. It's not the most ringing of endorsements – a glass-half-empty view – but it's still extremely significant and impactful.

I would argue that a more accurate description may be, "the best 'most probable outcome' alternative" – a glass-almost-full view.

Whether you see the glass as half empty or half full, making the right choice between VA and FIA income riders can mean the difference between having a client whose objectives and expectations have been met OR having a client who may have to settle for less than expected – or worse.

There are three steps to making a good decision:

1. Collect all of the available facts

2. Consider possible and probable factors that may influence those facts

3. Take action … or not (Inaction is also a decision)

Positive or negative, whatever happens after the decision is made won't change the fact that you made the best possible decision.

So, if we just look at the income rider portion of the VA or FIA choice, what are the facts you should consider to help your client make a good decision?

- FIA rollup percentages are routinely greater than those of VAs
- FIA payout percentages, on the income values, are higher than VAs
- If an FIA gives your client a higher, guaranteed income value AND pays a greater guaranteed percentage on that value, your client gets greater guaranteed lifetime income from a FIA!

Next, what other factors should you consider in your decision process?

Performance – VAs were designed to be performance engines. With a VA, it is argued that if the returns out-perform the rollups, the client benefits with higher-than-guaranteed income. That is true, but how likely is that to happen? With an assumed VA fee of 3.5 percent to overcome and a guaranteed rollup of 6 percent, how likely is it that a 9.5 percent return will be realized in a VA to actually increase the guaranteed income payout? Also, even though high returns can occur in a VA in any given year, the total return of the VA must overcome fees and exceed the rollup over the entire deferral period, not just in a given year!

The same thing can be said of FIAs. Though it's less likely to occur in an FIA than in a VA, it does happen. Case in point, I recently received policy statements on two clients whose five-year FIA performance has out-performed their rollup values.

Increasing income opportunity once income is elected – If your client considers income important now, won't it be even more important in the future – perhaps even critical? Increasingly, FIAs are offering clients income checks that increase and lock in as the selected indexes perform. While VAs may claim to offer opportunity here, evidence that this actually happens is not readily available.

Protection of the accumulated account value – While it is critical for our clients to plan, the best-laid plans don't always work out or reach fruition. If everything goes well (glass half full) and the market cooperates, your choice of either a VA or FIA with an income rider may not be that critical – they'll both perform, the income riders will kick in and perhaps the VA will even provide a little extra income due to long-term, solid subaccount performance.

BUT ... (glass half empty) if circumstances are such that your client can't wait the planned number of years to take income, and they need access to their account values NOW, poor market performance in the VA could result in a diminished account value or even one less than the original contract deposit. This would not happen in a FIA.

Winning Strategy: An FIA provides greater guaranteed income – that can be structured to increase – as well as an account value protected from negative market performance. A VA could potentially provide a somewhat higher guaranteed income and a fluctuating account value. So, what's your decision? An FIA? VA? A combination of both?

Ever Consider In-Service Withdrawals?
By Ryan McGee - December 15, 2014

I realize you've heard about the opportunity with baby boomers more than a thousand times, but it's vital that boomers be adequately prepared for retirement. With one misstep, years of planning could be jeopardized. Not safeguarding their life's work from a market downturn while transitioning into retirement could be devastating.

Your clients' 401(k)s need some level of principal protection and now may be the perfect opportunity to educate them about aged-based, in-service withdrawals at market highs. The strategy works by completing a direct rollover with a portion of their employer's retirement plan into a fixed index annuity within an Individual Retirement Account.

Keep in mind the IRS allows age-based, in-service withdrawals; however, each plan may have its own particular restrictions. In some cases, withdrawals may be based on service credits or subject to a vesting schedule. The benefits of an in-service withdrawal include more control over assets, additional income and wealth transfer options and the opportunity for more investment strategies.

It may be the perfect time for this strategy, considering history and today's market levels. Take a look at the S&P 500 index, for example. In the last 14 years, the S&P was nearly cut in half twice. According to the Federal Reserve, U.S. median household net worth decreased by 39 percent between 2007 and 2010, consequently reducing 18 years of gains during that time period.

Winning Strategy: Help protect your clients' nest eggs and create the retirement lifestyle they hoped for. Talk to your boomer clients about the possibility of age-based, in-service withdrawals.

Don't Let Clients Settle for Inefficiency
By Steve Pilger - November 27, 2014

The first advisor your client is going to call after they've been in a personal injury accident is likely their lawyer – not you. Don't be offended. However, it's important that you let them know you have the power to help make a big difference in the outcome of their case.

The average person's knowledge of structured settlements likely comes from horrible weekday afternoon TV commercials. That's because most people don't want to think about being involved in a personal injury, wrongful death, workers' compensation or other claims case. However, it's important to understand that these annuitized options can make a significant difference for your clients – whether they're claimants or defendants.

In addition to the guaranteed payment stream a structured settlement provides, there are several advantages:

- For the claimant, payments are exempt from federal and state income taxes
- For the defendant, the arrangement transfers full responsibility of future payments to an independent third party
- Structured settlements improve case resolution times – potentially reducing overhead costs and outside legal fees

Winning Strategy: If your clients are involved in a large claims case, make sure they know they have options.

Retirement: A Simple Math Problem

By Steve Schankerman - April 27, 2014

Most clients think retirement is a complicated process. You can help them make retirement simple with these easy steps:

Step 1: Identify their desired retirement income and years until their retirement date

Step 2: Calculate their Social Security income based on retirement date

Step 3: Subtract their desired income from their Social Security benefit – this number is the number you need to concentrate on

Step 4: Use a guaranteed income product to provide their needed income at retirement

Winning Strategy: Social Security only pays so much. Help your client secure another portion of their retirement income with an annuity.

Retirement for Savers AND Investors

By Steve Schankerman - November 20, 2014

In today's financial environment, what would it take to generate $10,000 in annual income? I see two main consumer categories here: savers and investors.

Savers

The savers aren't risk takers, and they focus mainly on fixed products. The risk for the saver is the uncertainty of future rates. Looking at the current average rates from bankrate.com, let's see what lump sum would be required to generate $10,000 of annual income.

Strategy	Interest Rate	Lump Sum Needed
1-year CD	.26%	$3,846,153
5-year CD	.83%	$1,204,819
5-year annuity	2.30%	$434,783
10-year treasury note	2.34%	$427,350

Investors

Now, let's look at an investor who may have a combination of fixed, bond and equity investments. Assuming a higher rate of return than the fixed products, the lump sum required for them is even smaller. But even though they need less money up front compared to the savers, investors risk the uncertainty of rate of return and longevity.

Alternatives

Here are two alternatives that eliminate return and longevity risks AND require smaller lump sums:

1. A fixed index annuity with an income rider would need only $181,818 to generate $10,000 a year for a 65-year-old

2. An immediate annuity would take approximately $160,000 to generate $10,000 a year with 10-year term certain for a 65-year-old

The income from these solutions would be guaranteed for the rest of the client's life, regardless of interest rates or how long they live.

Winning Strategy: You can secure your clients' retirement income many different ways. However, both savers and investors can benefit from annuity solutions … and they would potentially save money up front.

———————— ⌁ ————————

Fact or Fiction? You Be the Judge

By Michael Senkier - October 9, 2014

We've heard in the past that October is the biggest CD rollover month of the year – fact or fiction?

Let's look at some history. CDs were first sold in six-month increments (six months, 12 months, 18 months, etc.), but in October of 1983, they became deregulated.

Tax returns were a leading factor in the October/April trend. We saw an increase of CDs being established by people receiving a refund, or they surrendered their CDs to help pay for taxes due. At one point, Bank Rate Monitor estimated that upwards of $100 billion in CDs was in transition in each of those two months.

In order to smooth out the issuing of CDs and reduce the amount in play during October and April, banks started to offer them on odd terms, such as seven or 15 months. This slowly moved the trend across the balance of the year.

Look at today's CD rates on Bankrate.com (October 9, 2014):

- 1-year national average of .98%
- 2-year national average of 1.17%
- 5-year national average of 1.86%

Are CDs the right place for your clients? Or are you still following an outdated trend? The fact is, October is no longer one of the two hottest months for CD rollovers. It's open season throughout the year.

Winning Strategy: If your clients are looking for …

- Protection of principal
- Security from negative market fluctuation
- Tax deferral
- Penalty-free access to a portion of account value each year
- Opportunity to create guaranteed income for life

… Make sure you look at annuities as an option for their retirement plan.

—————————— ⟨◯⟩ ——————————

Myth, Busted

By Bill Stutz - December 8, 2014

It's an old rule of thumb (emphasis on the word old) that investors shouldn't buy annuities in their retirement accounts. It was a good rule when tax deferral was the only goal. But these days, clients most often buy annuities for their retirement income or principal guarantees – these guarantees can make sense anywhere clients are worried about their retirement assets, including IRAs.

The guarantees might either provide for current guaranteed income or secure a guaranteed base of lifetime income for future distributions.

In fact, it appears consumers were already figuring out the irrelevance of the "don't buy annuities inside of retirement accounts" rule all by themselves. According to LIMRA, in 2012 more than 60 percent of deferred variable and fixed indexed annuity purchases were being funded with IRA dollars!

Similarly, the emergence of guaranteed living benefit riders on fixed indexed annuities has arguably made them even more popular as a potential fit within retirement accounts, both for the risk/return characteristics of the annuity as an investment and the guaranteed income features for retirement income.

Nonetheless, the reality — as evidenced by the incredibly high election rate for buyers of annuities with guaranteed living benefit riders, and the rise of fixed indexed annuities as well — is that the majority of annuity purchases are still about buying access to guarantees and/or for unique investment opportunities (e.g., the risk/return profile of an equity-indexed annuity or a compelling yield in a fixed annuity). They're NOT for tax deferral!

Winning Strategy: Given these changes, it is perhaps time to abolish the "annuities should never go into an IRA" rule and recognize that it has become more a myth than sound advice in today's environment.

───────── ⌀ ─────────

Look Beyond the Numbers for Pension Risk Transfer
By Steve Pilger - January 12, 2016

No doubt, pension risk transfer activity is growing. Companies of all sizes, sectors and locations are shifting risk off their books to eliminate pension obligations. According to a study by the Pension Benefit Guaranty Corporation, between 2009 and 2013, more than 500 defined benefit plans transferred $67 billion of risk through lump-sum distributions and annuity purchases.[1]

If you have clients who are business owners, executives or professionals, e.g., doctors, dentists or lawyers, chances are they have a defined benefit pension plan. Although many of these plans have been replaced in recent years by 401(k) or other contributory plans, defined benefit plans remain a liability on a company's books. Plan sponsors face important decisions to address rising costs, increased regulation and uncertain market conditions.

Pension risk transfer can make sense for both parties – plan sponsors typically want to strengthen their balance sheet and ensure employees receive their retirement benefits, and insurance companies are in the business of investing and administering retiree liabilities.

This solution may not work for every situation, however. Many frozen pension plans lack sufficient assets to complete a transfer. These underfunded plans need help adjusting their investment strategy to close the gap between asset value and pension benefit obligation.

When selecting an annuity provider for pension risk transfer, plan sponsors have more to consider than corporate financial and competitive pricing. They should also factor in whether the provider:

- Will provide comprehensive customer service during and after plan transfer
- Offers retirement education for employees
- Responds to participant concerns

Winning Strategy: Now is an excellent time for you to offer pension risk transfer solutions that meet your clients' needs and fulfill commitments made to plan participants.

---

[1] *Risk Transfer Study, Pension Benefit Guaranty Corporation, December 2015.*

Afterword

By Larry Dahl, President of Ash Brokerage

As you likely know, one of the most elusive, yet important, indicators of an organization's success is its culture. Your company's culture defines what it is and what it can become. At Ash Brokerage, we are all stewards of our culture because we know it's our most valuable asset.

This book is a tangible example of our culture in action. We genuinely care about people and want to positively impact individuals, families, businesses and charities across America. Which is why we want to share our passion with you.

To be an authentic leader in the protection, retirement and longevity business, you absolutely need to be a thought leader. We take this responsibility very seriously. Properly and professionally addressing these issues requires an open sharing of ideas. It also requires thoughtful, reasoned and constructive dialogue around these very important – actually, acutely critical – topics that are relevant to everyone in the country. We are committed to using any channels we can to get the word out.

As our country's demographics change, we want to lead our industry to change as well. Every day, we make sure we have the right people in the right seats on the bus. And, we also make sure we have the right people driving the bus. One of those drivers, Mike McGlothlin, possesses a special talent and skill set – he is a caring and compassionate leader for our people and a compelling and creative thought leader for our industry. Just as he's been the driving force behind our blogs and this book, he has driven his team and our clients to incredible new heights.

We are proud of our entire Ash Brokerage team and the financial professionals we serve and partner with. We sincerely believe we can, and we will, profoundly impact – in a collaborative and client-centric manner – the thoughts and actions of people like you, the best financial advisors and protection specialists in America.

Leadership is a challenging, and often times daunting, responsibility. We humbly and gratefully accept the challenge of helping you and your clients think about, plan for and actually enjoy retirement – which is why we are committed to helping you plan for and address life's realities. Our ultimate goal is to create a foundation that addresses life's uncertainties and allows businesses and charities to thrive, and individuals and families to enjoy fulfilling and generous lives.

We hope you read this book with an active mind, thinking not only about how you can impact your business and your clients, but also your family, friends and community. We invite you to share what you've learned with others, and also share your thoughts, comments and suggestions with our team. Because, collectively, we have an incredible opportunity to guide people toward a financially stable and intentionally fulfilling and purposeful life. Let's do it together and create a powerful impact!

Made in the USA
Middletown, DE
24 April 2016